THE
MATURING CHRISTIAN
AND HIS ENEMIES

THE
MATURING
CHRISTIAN
AND HIS ENEMIES

WARREN RUSHTON

The Maturing Christian and His Enemies. Copyright © 2019 by Warren Rushton. All rights reserved. No part of this book may be used or reproduced in any manner whatsoever without written permission from the author, except in the case of brief quotations embodied in critical articles or reviews.

Print ISBN: 978-1-7323526-9-8
E-Book ISBN: 978-1-7330085-3-2

Library of Congress Control Number: 2019940449

Published in the United States of America by the Write Place, Inc.
For more information, please contact:

the Write Place, Inc.
809 W. 8th Street, Suite 2
Pella, Iowa 50219
www.thewriteplace.biz

Cover design by Lexie Thomas and interior design by Michelle Stam, the Write Place, Inc.

Cover scroll image 1367226503, shutterstock.com.
Cover painting by D' LaVon Armstrong.

Copies of this book may be ordered online at Amazon and BarnesandNoble.com.

View other Write Place titles at www.thewriteplace.biz.

DEDICATION

This book is dedicated to Chuck Evans, a
gifted evangelist and my father in the Faith.

TABLE OF CONTENTS

INTRODUCTION xiii
    The Importance of this Book.. xiii
    The Theological Neglect of the Subject xiv
    The Biblical Approach of this Book.............................. xv
    The Purpose of this Book xv

PART ONE: THE SPIRITUAL CONFLICT OF THE MATURING CHRISTIAN 17

CHAPTER 1: THE CHRISTIAN'S DEFENSE AGAINST THE FLESH 19
    The Meaning of the Word *Flesh* 19
    The Source of the Flesh.. 22
    The Strength of the Flesh 23
    The Defense Against the Flesh 27
    The Opposition of the Holy Spirit................................ 27
    The Responsibility of the Christian 29
        The Walk by the Holy Spirit.................................... 31
        The Quenching of the Holy Spirit 34

 The Grieving of the Holy Spirit 38
The Works of the Flesh 40
 Adultery (μοιεχία—*Moicheia*) 42
 Fornication (πορνεία—*Porneia*) 44
 Uncleanness (ἀκαθαρσία—*Akatharsia*) 45
 Lasciviousness (ἀσέλγεια—*Aselgeia*) 45
 Idolatry (εἰδωλολατρία—*Eidōlolatria*) 47
 Witchcraft (φαρμακεία—*Pharmakeia*) 47
 Hatred (ἔχθραι—*Echthrai*) 49
 Variance (ἔρις—*Eris*) 50
 Emulations (ζῆλος—*Zelos*) 52
 Wrath (θυμοί—*Thumoi*) 52
 Strife (ἐριθεῖαι—*Eritheiai*) 53
 Seditions (διχοστασίαι—*Dichostasia*) 55
 Heresies (αἱρέσεις—*Haireseis*) 55
 Envyings (φθόνου—*Phthovou*) 56
 Murders (φόνοι—*Phonoi*) 56
 Drunkenness (μέθαι—*Methai*) 57
 Revellings (κῶμοι—*Kōmoi*) 59
 The Like Things 60
The Fruit of the Spirit 62
 Love (ἀγάπη—*Agapē*) 63
 Joy (χαρά—*Chara*) 64
 Peace (εἰρήνη—*Eirēnē*) 66
 Longsuffering (μακροθυμία—*Makrothumia*) 67
 Gentleness (χρηστότης—*Chrēstotēs*) 67
 Goodness (ἀγαθωσύνη—*Agathōsunē*) 69
 Faith (πίστις—*Pistis*) 69

Meekness (πραΰτης—*Prautēs*) 71
Temperance (ἐγκράτεια—*Enkrateia*) 73

CHAPTER 2: THE CHRISTIAN'S DEFENSE AGAINST THE DEVIL 81
The Motive of the Devil 82
The Temptations of the Devil 83
  The Nature of the Temptations 84
    The wiles of the devil 86
    The devices of the devil 87
    The snare of the devil 88
  The Purpose of the Temptations 91
  The Identification of the Temptations 92
    Pride 93
    Age conforming or independence from God 93
    Worry 95
    Discouragement 97
    Cowardice in spiritual things 99
    Stealing 101
    Lying 102
    Laziness in spiritual things 104
    Tale bearing 105
    Busybody 105
    An unforgiving spirit 106
The Defenses for Satanic Temptations 107
  The Purpose of the Defenses 108
  The Nature of the Defenses 109
  The Armor of God 110
    The girdle of truth 113

- *The breastplate of righteousness* 114
- *The Gospel shoes* 116
- *The shield of faith* 117
- *The helmet of salvation* 118
- *The sword of the Spirit* 129
- The Place of Prayer and Supplication 130
- The Sober-Minded Christian 131

CHAPTER 3: THE CHRISTIAN'S DEFENSE AGAINST THE WORLD 137
- The Meaning of the Word *World* 137
  - The Created Universe 138
  - The Earth 138
  - The Unsaved 139
  - The System Controlled by Satan 140
- The Christian's Relationship to the World 149
  - The Use of the World 149
  - The Abuse of the World 151
- The Temptations of the World 153
  - The Lust of the Flesh 153
  - The Lust of the Eyes 155
  - The Pride of Life 155
- The Defenses for Worldly Temptations 157
  - Be Discerning 158
  - Refuse to Love the World 160

PART TWO: SPIRITUAL MATURITY IN RELATIONSHIP TO SPIRITUAL CONFLICT 165

CHAPTER 4: THE BASIS OF SPIRITUAL MATURITY 167
   The Spirit-Controlled Christian.................................... 168
      Sin.. 171
      Confession and Forgiveness..................................... 172
   The Spiritually Maturing Christian................................ 173
      The Need for Temptation 179
      The Need for Time 182
      The Need for the Word of God.................................... 183

CHAPTER 5: THE EFFECT OF SPIRITUAL MATURITY 189
   The Realization of the Simplicity of the Christian Life ... 189
      An Understanding of Grace... 193
      An Understanding of Dispensationalism 195
   The Realization of True Spiritual Service..................... 198
      The Priesthood of the Believer....................................200
      The Proper Use of Spiritual Gifts 202
      The Scriptural Type of Witness 204

CONCLUSION..207

BIBLIOGRAPHY 211
   A. Texts and Versions... 211
   B. Grammars and Lexicons.. 211
   C. Books and Commentaries... 214
   D. Periodical and Encyclopedia Articles 223
   E. Unpublished Materials... 224

Custom without truth is error grown old.

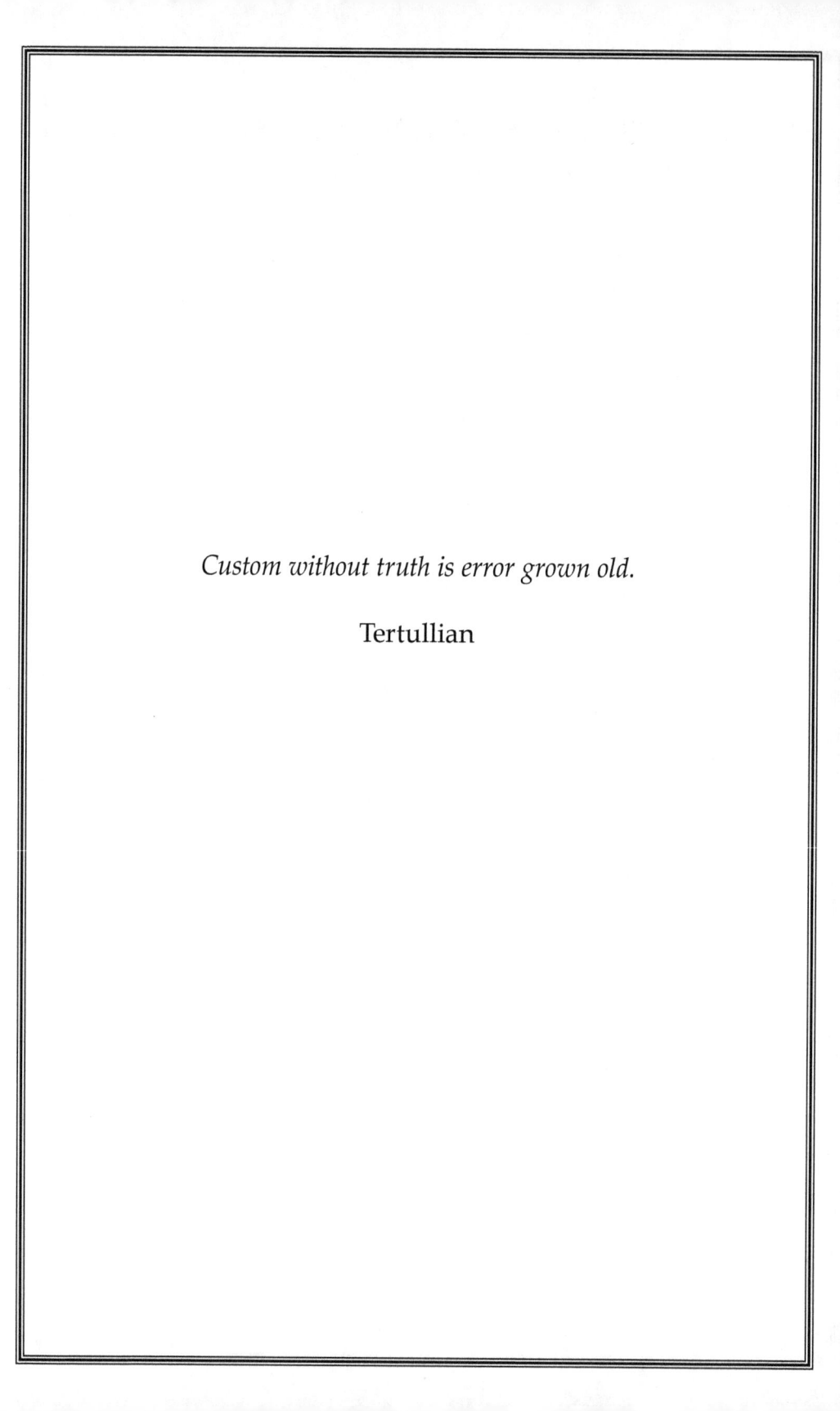

Tertullian

INTRODUCTION

It shall greatly help ye to understand the Scriptures if thou mark not only what is spoken or written, but of whom and to whom, with what words, at what time, where, to what intent, with what circumstances, considering what goeth before and what followeth after.

Miles Coverdale

The Importance of this Book

The importance of spiritual maturity cannot be stressed enough today. The Spirit-controlled life is the only life pleasing to God. Any righteous walk motivated by a source other than the Holy Spirit is merely the *bond woman's son,* dressed in the clothes of the *son of promise,* and is an insult to God.

For it is written, that Abraham had two sons, the one by a bondmaid, the other by a freewoman.²³ But he who was of the bondwoman was born after the flesh; but he of the freewoman was by promise. (Galatians 4:22-23).

Like many of the believers at Ephesus who *used curious arts,* many Christians today are trusting in spiritual rabbits' feet and false mysticism in a zealous effort to be spiritual.

And this was known to all the Jews and Greeks also dwelling at Ephesus; and fear fell on them all, and the name of the Lord Jesus was magnified.¹⁸ And many that believed came, and confessed, and shewed their deeds.¹⁹ Many of them also which used curious arts brought their books together, and burned them before all men: and they counted the price of them, and found it fifty thousand pieces of silver. (Acts 19: 17-19).

The Theological Neglect of the Subject

The spiritual life is a subject that will always gain a hearing and will usually produce some erroneous teaching. The reason for the former is that multitudes of Christians are living their lives with only a measure of victory. Their lives are symbolized by the rollercoaster, filled with expected ups and downs with no relief in sight as they observe the circular track. They are longing for a steady path of growth upward. Thus, they are willing to listen to almost any teacher who promises a way of escape. The reasons for considerable error in reference to the spiritual life are twofold. First, there is a general misunderstanding of what the normal spiritual life is; second, there is usually little accurate teaching concerning the spiritual enemies of the Christian and the appropriate defenses against them.

The Biblical Approach of this Book

The approach of this study will be Biblically based. The inerrant Scriptures are considered the only and final authority on the subject of the spiritual life; it is God alone who planned the acceptable approach to Himself! The terminology used in this book will be derived from the Bible. This, of course, rules out philosophical concepts and psychological terms that often are imposed on the Scriptures. This book also hopes to be free from the ever-popular individualistic theology and terminology of spiritual life practitioners, who go about hawking their wares from church to church, *while enriching themselves.*

The Purpose of this Book

The main purpose of this book is to show the relationship of the believer's enemies (and the necessary defenses against them) to Christian maturity. The tested from the Scriptures is that a Christian must know (1) his enemies and the temptations of each and (2) the defenses against each enemy and temptation, which must be in place before he can live a consistently growing Christian life and thus become a spiritually mature Christian.

Another important concern of this book is practicality. It should not be understood that the book will not be theological; anything that is truly practical for the child of God must first be doctrinal. This book will provide an exposition of key Biblical passages with applications that are of practical help to those who are finding it difficult to live a consistent Christian life before God and man.

PART ONE

THE SPIRITUAL CONFLICT OF THE MATURING CHRISTIAN

No man can quench his thirst with sand, or with water from the Dead Sea; so no man can find rest from his own character, however good, or from his own acts, however religious.

Horatius Bonar

CHAPTER 1

THE CHRISTIAN'S DEFENSE AGAINST THE FLESH

There are only three enemies that can cause a Christian to lose fellowship with God. These are *the flesh, the devil,* and *the world.* The enemy that is constantly with the Christian and of which he is most aware is the flesh.

The Meaning of the Word *Flesh*

Flesh is used several different ways in the Bible. Some are as follows:
1. It is used of all mankind.
   As thou hast given him power over all flesh, that he should give eternal life to as many as thou hast given him. (John 17:2).

2. It is used of all creatures.
And the LORD said, I will destroy man whom I have created from the face of the earth; both man, and beast, and the creeping thing, and the fowls of the air; for it repenteth me that I have made them. (Genesis 6:17).

And all flesh died that moved upon the earth, both of fowl, and of cattle, and of beast, and of every creeping thing that creepeth upon the earth, and every man… (Genesis 7:21).

3. It is used of meat on the bones.
Behold my hands and my feet, that it is I myself: handle me, and see; for a spirit hath not flesh and bones, as ye see me have. (Luke 24:39).

4. It is used of human nature.
And the Word was made flesh, and dwelt among us, (and we beheld his glory, the glory as of the only begotten of the Father,) full of grace and truth. (John 1:14).

For I could wish that myself were accursed from Christ for my brethren, my kinsmen according to the flesh… (Romans 9:3).

5. It is used of the days of Christ's earthly ministry.
Who in the days of his flesh, when he had offered up prayers and supplications with strong crying and tears

unto him that was able to save him from death, and was heard in that he feared... (Hebrews 5:7).

6. It is used of lineage.
   Whose are the fathers, and of whom as concerning the flesh Christ came, who is over all, God blessed for ever. Amen. (Romans 9:5).

7. It is used of a person.
   For if the blood of bulls and of goats, and the ashes of an heifer sprinkling the unclean, sanctifieth to the purifying of the flesh... (Hebrews 9:13).

8. It is used of the humanity of Christ.
   For many deceivers are entered into the world, who confess not that Jesus Christ is come in the flesh. This is a deceiver and an antichrist. (2 John 1:7).

9. It is used as the sin principle within every person.
   Now the works of the flesh are manifest, which are these; Adultery, fornication, uncleanness, lasciviousness... (Galatians 5:19).

The word *flesh* has an often-used synonym in the Scriptures: *sin*. *Flesh* lays emphasis on the location of the monster within each of us. The words *the sin* lay emphasis on the fact that the old nature desires to throw off God's restraints (Romans 7:7-11). It is called *indwelling sin* in Romans 7:17.[1] There is nothing good in the flesh.

> *For I know that in me (that is, in my flesh,) dwelleth no good thing: for to will is present with me; but how to perform that which is good I find not. (Romans 7:18).*

The flesh never became remolded at salvation. There is no self-improvement program for the flesh enjoined in the Scriptures. The word *flesh* then, as it relates to the spiritual life, is that sin nature that has been characteristic of mankind since Adam begat men in his image and his own likeness.

> *And Adam lived an hundred and thirty years, and begat a son in his own likeness, after his image; and called his name Seth… (Genesis 5:3).*

The Source of the Flesh

The modern behaviorist views the ills of mankind by suggesting there has not been enough time for evolution to rid man of evil animal propensities.[2] This concept, however, is foreign to the Bible. The Scriptures teach that the fall was downward and not a gradual climb upward (Romans 5:12).[3] They trace physical death to mankind's relationship to Adam, and in a similar Romans 5:21[4] traces spiritual death as a result of *the sin* (ἡ ἁμαρτία). Many were constituted sinners because of the disobedience of one man, and that one man in Romans 5 is Adam. The result of a fallen nature is seen in Adam's first son, for he killed his brother, Abel. The Bible terms *the flesh* this continual bent to do unrighteous things. The connection to the source of the corruption is called *the old man*.

> *Knowing this, that our old man is crucified with him, that the body of sin might be destroyed, that henceforth we should not serve sin. (Romans 6:6).*

> *Lie not one to another, seeing that ye have put off the old man with his deeds... (Colossians 3:9).*

The works wrought from the old man are the works of the flesh. The thrust of Scripture, in reference to the flesh, is that it is here to stay as long as there is life on earth; even worse, there is nothing a Christian can do himself to break with the old man or curb completely the works of the flesh.

> *For I know that in me (that is, in my flesh,) dwelleth no good thing: for to will is present with me; but how to perform that which is good I find not. (Romans 7:18).*

The Strength of the Flesh

Ovid (Metamorphoses 7.20) uttered his famous sigh of frustration: Video meliora, proboque; Deteriora sequor.

"I see the better things, and I agree with them, but I follow the worse."

"Men," said Seneca, "love and hate their vices at the same time." (Letters 112. 3)...

What then is the reason for this warfare? Wherein lies the power of the evil force?[5]

Paul says:

Wretched man that I am: who shall deliver me from the body of this death? (Romans 7:24).

The strength of the sin that lies within the bosom of every Christian ought to offer admonishment so that each one would *take heed unto thyself* (1 Timothy 4:16).

The classic passage which proves that the new nature cannot control the old is Romans 7:15-24. L. S. Chafer has copied this text with brackets to indicate the natures.

For that which I [the old] do I [the new] allow not: for what I [the new] would, that do I [the old] not; but what I [the new] hate, that do I [the old]. If then I [the old] do that which I [the new] would not, I consent unto the law or will of God for me that it is good. Now then it is no more I [the new] that do it, but sin [the old] that dwelleth in me. For I know that in me *[the old]* (that is, in my flesh), dwelleth no good thing: for to will is present with me; but how to perform that which is good I find not. For the good that I *[the new]* would I *[the old]* do not: but the evil which I *[the new]* would not, that I *[the old]* do. Now if I *[the old]* do that I *[the new]* would not, it is no more I *[the new]* that do it, but sin *[the old]* that dwelleth in me. I find then a law *[not a law of Moses]*, that, when I *[the new]* would do good, evil *[the old]* is present with me. For I delight in the law of God after the inward man: but I see another law in my members *[the old]*, warring against the law of my mind *[the new]*, that delights in the law of God, and bringing me into captivity to the law, of sin *[the old]* which is in my members. O wretched Christian man that I am: who shall deliver me from the body of this death?[6] (Romans 7: 15-24).*

Many have made the observation that the Holy Spirit is not mentioned at all in Romans 7, and thus there is no victory; however, Romans 8 refers to the Holy Spirit more than any other chapter in the New Testament. It should be noted that the strength of the flesh is primarily seen when one work is called into question. For example, not every Christian out of fellowship with God is a drunkard or a fornicator. The laws of the land or social pressure may be the agents that curb these particular works of the flesh. The point is there are some works of the flesh peculiar to that person that no restraint humanly devised can control. Murder is a capital crime, yet it is committed many times every day in the world. Works of the flesh and their relative control at any one time depend (while the believer is out of fellowship) on the flesh work motivated to action. Paul says:

> *But sin, taking occasion by the commandment, wrought in me all manner of concupiscence (strong desires, επιθυμίαν). For without the law sin was dead. (Romans 7:8).*

Paul's sin principle was brought to life by a law principle. The law called in question the flesh and the law by itself had no power over the flesh:

> *For what the law could not do, in that it was weak through the flesh, God sending his own Son in the likeness of sinful flesh, and for sin, condemned sin in the flesh… (Romans 8:3).*

The man living in immorality in 1 Corinthians 5:1 was weak in at least this one area, but there is no indication that he or any of the Corinthians were guilty of sorcery. Yet they were quite capable of such in their carnal state. However, some of the believers at Ephesus were guilty of sorcery, as Acts 19:17-19 indicates. The flesh is so ingrained into a person's makeup and personality that the type and strength of works of the flesh can be indicated by the flesh habits an individual has indulged in before or after salvation, because all works of the flesh are addictive to some degree.

The Defense Against the Flesh

The defense against the flesh differs in kind from the defenses against the devil or the world. The defense against the flesh is not a matter of directing one's love or putting on armor, but rather relying upon the ministry of the Holy Spirit, who opposes the works of the flesh. The new nature that a Christian has is no match for the strength of the flesh. God Himself must step in and control the flesh. This He does when we order our life by His leading and the opposing action is complete and perfect.

The Opposition of the Holy Spirit

The Christian has the promise that if he walks by the Spirit, he will by no means (οὐ μὴ ensures the absoluteness of it) bring to completion a strong desire (ἐπιθυμίαν) of the flesh (Galatians 5:16). The need for such absolute control of the strong desires is given in verse 17:

> *For the flesh lusteth against the Spirit, and the Spirit against the flesh: and these are contrary the one to the other: so that ye cannot do the things that ye would. (Galatians 5:17).*

The γὰρ in verse 17 definitely links these two verses by way of explanation. When a Christian is walking by the Holy Spirit, the Spirit places Himself in an absolute opposing force against the flesh, so that it is impossible for a Christian to give vent to the works of his flesh. The opposition keeps the believer from doing the things his sin nature would desire. The word *contrary* is ἀντίκειται. This word is used in 2 Thessalonians 2:4[7] in reference to the one who opposes God. It is used in 1 Timothy 1:10 in reference to anything that is contrary or opposing sound doctrine. Wuest says of this word in the context of Galatians 5:17:

> The words "are contrary" are from antikeimai which means "to lie opposite to," hence "to oppose, withstand." The words "the one to the other," are from *allelos*, a reciprocal pronoun in Greek. Thus, there is a reciprocity on the part of the flesh and Spirit.[8]

Galatians 5:16-17,[9] in this writer's opinion, is one of the greatest promises to the maturing Christian. It relieves one of any and all self-efforts in controlling the flesh and places the burden upon the One who Scripturally takes full responsibility. This truth teaches another truth that is perhaps less obvious: When a believer is walking by the Holy Spirit, the sin that breaks fellowship with God does not come from a work of the flesh. The logical conclusion is profound in its far-reaching implications. Since a Christian has only three enemies—namely the flesh, the devil, and the world—only the devil and the world can produce temptations that can result in broken fellowship. The Spirit-walking Christian can take his attention from his sin nature and assume a new responsibility.

The Responsibility of the Christian

While a Christian is walking by means of the Spirit, the works of the flesh are under control. They will not be brought to completion. It should not be understood that the flesh is eradicated, dead, or even dormant. While the believer is in fellowship with God, the flesh is very much alive and always ready to fulfill its strong desires. While a Christian cannot fulfill the lusts of the flesh in this relationship (Galatians 5:16), he should be aware of all of the works of the flesh to determine and discern his true position.

> *But he that is spiritual judgeth all things, yet he himself is judged of no man. (1 Corinthians 2:15).*

This verse says it is impossible to discern a spiritual man, but it is not difficult to judge when one is not because the works of the flesh are manifest. It should be remembered that the only thing the flesh can do is produce its works. The flesh does not tempt one to act independently of God, for it will do that whenever it is not controlled. The flesh is always at enmity with God. It is not subject to the law of God.

Because the carnal mind is enmity against God: for it is not subject to the law of God, neither indeed can be. (Romans 8:7).

It is not the responsibility of the Christian to control the flesh, for he cannot.

For the good that I would I do not: but the evil which I would not, that I do. (Romans 7:19)

It is the responsibility of the child of God to order his life by the Holy Spirit of God. For example, a person who drank considerably before he was saved may feel the desire to drink, perhaps at an office party. If this Christian is walking by the Spirit, this desire cannot be brought to completion. For the sake of argument, suppose this believer did succumb to his desire of the flesh and got stone drunk. A possible explanation of the events could be as follows: (1) When he got drunk, he was not walking by the Spirit, because drunkenness is a work of the flesh; (2) There had to have been a temptation from the world or from the devil to take him from the place of fellowship, and thus remove the Holy Spirit's ministry of suppressing the work of the flesh—drunkenness; (3) The reason it had to be either the world or Satan is that sin is the only thing that can break fellowship.

If we say that we have fellowship with him, and walk in darkness, we lie, and do not the truth:[7] But if we walk in the light, as he is in the light, we have fellowship one with another, and the blood of Jesus Christ his Son cleanseth us from all sin.[8] If we say that we have no sin, we deceive ourselves, and the truth is not in us.[9] If we confess our sins, he is faithful and just to forgive us our sins, and to cleanse us from all unrighteousness. (1 John 1:6-9).

And no acts of the flesh can come into being while a believer is under the Spirit's control (Galatians 5: 16); (4) Perhaps someone at the party teased him or put him in a position where Satan planted the thought of some form of pride; he fell for this, acted independently of God, and stopped depending upon the leading and guiding ministry of the Holy Spirit. The Spirit-walking Christian then must be very sober and know his enemies well.

THE WALK BY THE HOLY SPIRIT

Galatians 5: 16 states:

This I say then, Walk in (by means of) the Spirit, and ye shall not fulfill the lust of the flesh.

What is meant by the expression, *Walk by the Spirit?* The word *walk* is περιπατεῖτε. This word means in a literal sense *to walk*. Here it is used metaphorically and means sphere of conduct.[10] Vine says the word signifies "the whole round of the activities of the individual life."[11] It is "the act of conducting one's self, or ordering one's manner of life or behavior."[12]

A Christian should govern his whole life by the Spirit of God. περιπατεῖτε is a present imperative, which visualizes this walk as something continuous. It should not be considered as merely good advice, but rather as a command. The believer is the subject of this active verb and emphasizes the fact that the child of God has the responsibility of ordering his life by means of the Holy Spirit. The control or filling of the Holy Spirit (Ephesians 5:18), which will be discussed in Chapter 4, looks at the same condition (as walking by the Spirit), but considers the situation from the viewpoint of what happens when a Christian is walking by the Spirit. *In the Spirit* is actually *by means of the Spirit*; πνεύματι should be understood as instrumental rather than locative. The Christian, then, is not left to perpetuate his own brand of piety. The Holy Spirit works through the believer to produce His fruit and manifest Christ-likeness.

> In no sense does the believer lead, or direct, the Spirit. He can, however, be dependent on the Spirit, and this is his exact responsibility as revealed in this passage.[13]

The question now is this: How is a believer to walk by the Spirit? How does one rely upon God to produce this continuous walk? The answer to this is not easy to explain. It is like explaining to someone how to believe. As they say, "There just ain't no knobs to twist, buttons to push, or beads to count that will do the trick." It is by faith. Just as a person believed certain and definite things (the Gospel) by an act of faith, likewise he believes certain and definite things that belong to the Christian life; he begins to live and walk by an attitude of faith. As a Christian feeds upon the doctrines of the Word of God, he will grow in grace. As he contemplates (thinks) upon his position in Christ, his spirit will grow more and more to appreciate this new life. By setting his affections on things above, his earthly life will reflect this affection. The importance of the Word of God cannot be overstressed in regard to walking by the Spirit, because this is the only source of knowledge of the content of salvation that a Christian has in his dispensation. So Paul requests in Ephesians 3:17-18:

That Christ may dwell in your hearts by faith; that yet being rooted and grounded in love,[18] May be able to comprehend with all saints what is the breadth, and length, and depth, and height...

(Also Colossians 2:2-5 and Philippians 4:8.) This speaks of what a Christian has *in Christ*.

This attitude of thinking upon things above is the positive half of the continual reckoning oneself dead unto the sin nature, as stated in Romans 6:11.

The walk of a Christian is a very delicate thing, because the Holy Spirit can easily be quenched or grieved.

THE QUENCHING OF THE HOLY SPIRIT

First Thessalonians 5:18-20 states:

In every thing give thanks: for this is the will of God in Christ Jesus concerning you.[19] *Quench not the Spirit.*[20] *Despise not prophesyings.*

The quenching of the Spirit, as seen from these verses, relates very closely to accepting the will (Θέλω, *Thelo*) or desire of God and prophesyings—the revelation from God. Quenching means to render ineffective for the purpose intended. For example, the word is used in Hebrews 11:34, where it says the heroes of faith *quenched the violence of fire.* The word *violence* is δύναμιν, which could be translated *power* or *ability*. This is probably referring to the *three Hebrew children,* Haaaniah, Mishael, and Azariah (Jewish names), who King Nebuchadnezzar threw into the fiery furnace. The account reads:

And the princes, governors, and captains, and the king's counsellors, being gathered together, saw these men, upon whose bodies the fire had no power, nor was an hair of their head singed, neither were their coats changed, nor the smell of fire had passed on them. (Daniel 3:27).

Quenching the fire means it was stopped from completing its intended purpose. The same idea is true in reference to the Holy Spirit. His purpose for and ministry in a believer is rendered inoperative.

Since it is the Holy Spirit that intercedes for each Christian according to the will of the Father (Romans 8:27), all things work together for good (Romans 8:28), and the good is judged as being conformed to the Son of God (Romans 8:29).

> *And he that searcheth the hearts knoweth what is the mind of the Spirit, because he maketh intercession for the saints according to the will of God.[28] And we know that all things work together for good to them that love God, to them who are the called according to his purpose.[29] For whom he did foreknow, he also did predestinate to be conformed to the image of his Son, that he might be the firstborn among many brethren. (Romans 8:27-29).*

The conclusion is that a Christian can give thanks in everything that comes into his life—sin apart.

> Anytime the Christian does not rejoice or give thanks in everything, he is out of the will of God. That does not mean only in good circumstances, for even the natural man rejoices in enjoyable circumstances. But when the Scripture tells us "rejoice evermore" and "in everything give thanks," it means in any circumstance.[14]

The quenching of the Holy Spirit will come about initially from the devil or the world. These two enemies will always endeavor to lead the Christian in their way. so that they begin to stop the Holy Spirit's ministry of controlling the sin nature.

Suppose, for example, a Spirit-filled Christian is rejoicing in the Lord as he is driving down the freeway in his new automobile. Suddenly traffic rapidly slows down and comes to a standstill. While the believer's car is stopped, his car is smashed into from the rear by another car. Fortunately, no one is hurt, but his new car has suffered at least $10,000 in damage and the motorist at fault has no insurance. This Christian, upon realizing the situation, begins to speak sharply in anger to the other motorist. What actually happened?

One minute he was a Spirit-led Christian; a few moments later he was engulfed by a work of the flesh. The Christian should have given thanks to God for bringing this event into his life (1 Thessalonians 5:16). *Rejoice evermore.* But he did not! He therefore rendered the Spirit's ministry through him ineffective. Simultaneously, with this quenching attitude he perhaps entertained the thought (from Satan) to be proud of his new car. Satan, no doubt, couched it in such terms as, "You know God holds you accountable for acting as a good steward of His gifts. You had better see if you can't get that fellow to pay something. Put the pressure on; he'll give in." The Christian yields to this thought by a determined act of his will. Sin results with broken fellowship, which allows him to fulfill a work of the flesh—an outburst of anger.

Another activity that is closely linked with quenching the Spirit is despising prophesying. The word *despise* means to count as nothing or to *treat with contempt*.[15] Since prophesy came into existence by the *manifestation of the Spirit* (1 Corinthians 12:7, 10), He (the Holy Spirit) is very sensitive concerning the believer's attitude toward the Word of God. Some of the Thessalonian Christians were *treating with contempt* the giving forth of the Word of God. This is meaningful today by application only. Since the Word of God is complete, the gift of prophesy is not operative in the church.

> *Charity never faileth: but whether there be prophecies, they shall fail; whether there be tongues, they shall cease; whether there be knowledge, it shall vanish away.[9] For we know in part, and we prophesy in part.[10] But when that which is perfect is come, then that which is in part shall be done away.[11] When I was a child, I spake as a child, I understood as a child, I thought as a child: but when I became a man, I put away childish things.[12] For now we see through a glass, darkly; but then face to face: now I know in part; but then shall I know even as also I am known.[13] And now abideth faith, hope, charity, these three; but the greatest of these is charity. (1 Corinthians 13:8-13.)*

Prophesy does exist, however, in the written Word of God. Prophesying did not refer only to future events but to the complete revelation in Scripture.

Many Christians today would never question that the Bible is the inspired Word of God or pervert the Scriptures by their open denial of the plain and normal meaning of Scripture. Also, a believer who despises the proclamation of the Word is in grave danger of quenching the Spirit who energizes the one teaching the Scriptures. This type of closemindedness usually results in Satanic ensnarement in opposing the truth. If a child of God is not open to the Word in order to be illumined by the Holy Spirit, he will learn from the Bible just exactly what he has predetermined—nothing. But even worse, the Holy Spirit will be rendered inoperative in his life.

THE GRIEVING OF THE HOLY SPIRIT

There is only one passage that speaks of grieving the Holy Spirit, Ephesians 4:30:

> *And grieve not the Holy Spirit of God, whereby ye are sealed unto the day of redemption.*

In the context, Paul is talking about works of the flesh. In verses 29 and 31, he is speaking of those who misuse the mouth:

> *Let no corrupt communication proceed out of your mouth... Let all bitterness, and wrath, and anger, and clamor, and evil speaking be put away from you, with all malice.*

When these characteristics are present in a Christian's life, the Holy Spirit is grieved. God is a person and has feelings and emotions, so He can be grieved. Apparently, the Ephesians were allowing these works of the flesh, for the Greek text literally and emphatically states, *Stop grieving the Holy Spirit of God.*

The word *grieve* shows the personal concern and sensitivity of the Holy Spirit in reference to a believer's spiritual condition. The word *grieve* is λυπεῖτε and is translated *grieve* seven times, *sorrow* eighteen times, and *be in heaviness* once.[16] When the Lord repeatedly asked Peter, "Lovest thou me?" in John 21:17, the Scriptures state, *"Peter was grieved because he said unto him the third time, 'Lovest thou me?'"* Humanly, Peter felt he had let the Lord down, which he had. This reminder hurt him deeply.

In 1 Thessalonians 4:13, Paul introduces his sermon designed to comfort those who had lost loved ones by saying:

> *...that ye sorrow (grieve) not, even as others which have no hope.*

This sorrow is a mental attitude of a deep sense of loss and loneliness because of a departed loved one. When the Holy Spirit is grieved, He feels a deep hurt because His ministry of fruit production in the Christian and the manifestation of Christ through the believer must stop. The Spirit stops opposing the flesh, and man's sin nature is able to ride roughshod over the new nature; soon the works of the sin nature appear. When these works of the flesh soil the believer's testimony, the Spirit is surely grieved, for He longs again to produce His fruit. When fruit is not being produced by the Holy Spirit, then the flesh will be producing its works.

The Works of the Flesh

The works of the flesh are listed in the Book of Galatians:

> *Now the works of the flesh are manifest, which are these: Adultery, fornication, uncleanness, lasciviousness,[20] Idolatry, witchcraft, hatred, variance, emulations, wrath, strife, seditions, heresies,[21] Envyings, murders, drunkenness, revellings, and such like: of the which I tell you before, as I have also told you in time past, that they which do such things shall not inherit the kingdom of God. (Galatians 5:19-21).*

It is most important for the Christian to know from the Scriptures exactly what is involved in each work of the flesh, so he can detect them if and when they make an appearance. When a work of the flesh is detected, the Christian must realize immediately that it is time to confess, for fellowship has been broken because he is no longer walking by the Spirit.

> *This I say then, Walk in the Spirit, and ye shall not fulfil the lust of the flesh. (Galatians 5:16).*

The list of the works of the flesh has been divided into categories by some. Lightfoot says:

> Though no systematic classification is to be looked for in the catalogue which follows, yet a partial and

unconscious arrangement may perhaps be discerned. The sins here mentioned seem to fall into four classes: (1) Sensual passions, "fornication, uncleanness, licentiousness," (2) Unlawful dealings in things spiritual, "idolatry, witchcraft," (3) Violations of brotherly love, "enmities...murders," (4) Intemperate excesses, "drunkenness, revellings."[17]

Barclay makes the observation that the flesh works are perversions of good things:

It may be that here is the best point at which to note a grim fact about the works of the flesh. Without exception, every one of these is a perversion of something which is in itself good. Immorality, impurity, licentiousness are perversions of the sexual instinct which is in itself a lovely thing and part of love. Idolatry is a perversion of worship, and was begun as an aid to worship. Sorcery is a perversion of the use of healing drugs in medicine. Envy, jealousy, and strife are perversions of that noble ambition and desire to do well which can be a spur to greatness. Enmity and anger are a perversion of that righteous indignation without which the passion for goodness cannot exist. Dissension and the party spirit are a perversion of the devotion to principle which can produce the martyr. Drunkenness and carousing are the perversion of the happy joy of social fellowship and of the things which men can happily and legitimately enjoy. Nowhere is there better illustrated the power of evil to take beauty and to twist it into ugliness, to take the finest things and to make them an avenue for sin. The awfulness of the power of sin lies precisely in its ability to take the raw material of potential goodness and turn it into the material of evil.[18]

Paul begins by listing the works that plague society—sexual perversion.

ADULTERY (μοιεχία—*Moicheia*)

The word *adultery* occurs first in Exodus 20:14 in the Ten Commandments. No explanation of it is given. In Leviticus 20:10, there is enough context to give meaning to the word:

And the man that committeth adultery with another man's wife, even he that committeth adultery with his neighbor's wife, the adulterer and the adulteress shall surely be put to death; their blood shall be upon them.

Adultery means sexual intercourse by a married person with someone not his or her legitimate mate (John 8:3, 4; Matthew 19:9). The concept is emphasized by the figurative usage of the word. Israel is pictured as married to Jehovah, but the people went after other nations and turned to worshipping the gods of those nations; so, God says through the prophet:

> *And I saw, when for all the causes whereby backsliding Israel committed adultery I had put her away, and given her a bill of divorce; yet her treacherous sister Judah feared not, but went and played the harlot also. (Jeremiah 3:8).*

Adultery has generally been considered a deed punishable by law.

> In Gk. law μοιεχία is simply "secret sexual intercourse with a free woman without the consent of her (κύριος—*kurios*)." In face of such violation (ὕβρις) the husband or family (father, brother, son) has the right of private revenge (by killing, maltreatment, or fine).[19]

While this ancient law may have been on the books, it was certainly not written upon the hearts of the unregenerate Greek world. Sexual looseness came to be considered not a vice but an acceptable way of life.

> Roman women, says Seneca, were married to be divorced and were divorced to be married. Some of them distinguished the years, not by the names of the consuls, but by the names of their husbands.[20]

It was in this culture that the church started. The teaching of the Church Epistles went cross-grain to the existing culture, and it is stated in Galatians 5:21b, *that they which do such things shall not inherit the kingdom of God.*

FORNICATION (πορνεία—*Porneia*)

The English word *pornography* comes from this word, but it contains a larger concept. The word translated *fornication* means prostitution. The word came to mean sexual looseness outside of marriage. It is the overall term referring to this type of impurity. The case of incest in 1 Corinthians 5:1-7 is called fornication. Fornication includes any type of sexual perversion. For example, those in Sodom and Gomorrah are classified as fornicators.

> *Even as Sodom and Gomorrah, and the cities about them in like manner, giving themselves over to fornication, and going after strange flesh, are set forth for an example, suffering the vengeance of eternal fire. (Jude 7).*

Their perversion was going after strange (ἑτέρας—*heteras*) flesh. This work of the flesh is common to all nations and peoples. It is very similar to today's LGBTQ movement. This sin is running wild, and they are pushy just like they were with Lot in Genesis 19:5-11. Society may pass laws against adultery, but still fornication runs wild.

It should be noted that since every born-again Christian has the flesh with him, he is capable of fulfilling this work of fornication. His only sure protection against such a work is *walking by means of the Spirit*. It is possible to descend lower into moral corruption than adultery and fornication. The word *uncleanness* goes lower into the abyss of the sin nature.

UNCLEANNESS (ἀκαθαρσία—*Akatharsia*)

In literature outside the New Testament, ἀκαθαρσία refers to dirt that is removed when a tenant leaves a rented house.[21] The word ἀκαθαρσία is linked four times in the New Testament with fornication (Galatians 5:19; Ephesians 5:3; Colossians 3:5; Revelation 17:4). In Romans 1:24, *uncleanness* appears to be in apposition to *dishonor*. Then in Romans 1:26, *vile affections* are literally *passions of dishonor*. Thus, there is a close link between *uncleanness* and homosexuality. As the context indicates, the more a person turns from God, the more he will be turned to these unnatural (ἀκαθαρσία) works of the flesh.

Even further down is the word *lasciviousness*. Some states now are considering passing laws against talking about the sin of being gay. You will not be able to preach from the Bible in this area without be arrested and fined.

LASCIVIOUSNESS (ἀσέλγεια—*Aselgeia*)

The word *lasciviousness* is not in common usage today, even though this work of the flesh ranks high in popularity with the children of wrath heading toward the Great Lake.

And whosoever was not found written in the book of life was cast into the lake of fire. (Revelation 20:15).

ἀσέλγεια could be translated *debauchery*.²² It also, as in the American Standard Version, can be translated *lewdness*. These words still do not tell exactly the idea of this flesh work. Lightfoot says:

A man may be ἀκάθαρτος and hide his sin; he does not become ἀκάελγὴς until he shocks public decency.²³

The essence of this word is not anyone particular act of sexual perversion, but rather one's attitude toward the perversion.

It is completely indifferent to public opinion and to public decency. A man may well begin to do a wrong thing in secret; at the beginning his one aim and desire may be to hide it from the eyes of men. He may love the wrong thing, and he may even be mastered by it, but he is still ashamed of it. But it is perfectly possible for him to come to a stage when he does openly and blatantly that which he did secretly and in concealment. He may come to a stage of sin when he is so lost to shame that he no longer cares what others see, and what they may say, or what they may think.²⁴

The category of flesh works now goes from sexual perversion to religious perversion—idolatry and witchcraft.

IDOLATRY (εἰδωλολατρία—*Eidōlolatria*)

Idolatry is a transliteration of the Greek word εἰδωλολατρία and means to worship an idol that was originally meant to be an aid in worship to localize and visualize the god. When Paul came to Athens, he found the city full of images.

> *Now while Paul waited for them at Athens, his spirit was stirred in him, when he saw the city wholly given to idolatry. (Acts 17:16).*

In their ignorance, these people were attempting to worship gods by physical representations. To be religious in this way is by no means a spiritual thing; it is a work of the flesh. This activity of the flesh is very common in carnal Christians. An elaborate form of public worship is of utmost importance to them. A simple meeting, especially on Sunday morning, to hear the Word of God expounded, without the trappings of doxologies, long pulpit prayers, choir responses, etcetera, would severely offend their esthetic nature. They are not satisfied with the simplicity of breaking bread, having fellowship, and hearing the ministry of the Word. They must have the approved liturgy before they feel like they have been in church. A further perversion of religion is witchcraft.

WITCHCRAFT (φαρμακεία—*Pharmakeia*)

φαρμακεία is used two other times in the New Testament.

> *Neither repented they of their murders, nor of their sorceries, nor of their fornication, nor of their thefts. (Revelation 9:21).*
>
> *And the light of a candle shall shine no more at all in thee; and the voice of the bridegroom and of the bride shall be heard no more at all in thee: for thy merchants were the great men of the earth; for by thy sorceries were all nations deceived. (Revelation 18:23).*

Pharmakeia is a medical term and refers to the use of drugs. (The English word *pharmacy* is a derivative.) The reason the word came to mean witchcraft or sorcery is seen in the close association of drugs with religious superstitious awe.

Those who tamper in spiritism or witchcraft are not so much under the control of Satan as they are their own flesh nature. Satan and his demons no doubt use witchcraft to deceive people, but they do not produce it, for its source is the flesh. The Ephesian Christians, for a time, were taken in by this.

> *Many of them also which used curious arts brought their books together, and burned them before all men: and they counted the price of them, and found it fifty thousand pieces of silver. (Acts 19:19).*

When they finally realized this fact, they burnt their books of witchcraft. The growing use of horoscopes evidences a superstitious reverence on the part of many committed converts. This practice is not of faith, but of flesh.

HATRED (ἔχθραι—*Echthraí*)

The word ἔχθραι takes a person from the realm of religious perversion to emotional excesses. This word hardly needs to be explained, since examples of it are everywhere. One interesting observation can be made. The previous works are generally not tolerated in Christian circles, but emotional excesses are often passed over without a glance; yet they are all from the flesh. It is a sad situation when the dictates of society set the norm of tolerance for the church.

The word ἔχθραι, as seen in Luke 22:12, is the opposite of friendship:

> *And the same day Pilate and Herod were made friends together: for before they were at enmity between themselves.*

James 4:4 states:

> *Ye adulterers and adulteresses, know ye not that the friendship of the world is enmity with God?*

This type of hatred or set animosity is the direct opposite of the fruit of the Spirit—love.

VARIANCE (ἔρις—*Eris*)

Variance is a similar word to hatred and basically means contention or strife. ἔρις is used in four other places in the Church Epistles. The unsaved world is guilty of strife.

> *Being filled with all unrighteousness, fornication, wickedness, covetousness, maliciousness; full of envy, murder, debate, deceit, malignity; whisperers... (Romans 1:29).*

Strife is listed as a work of the flesh in which Christians are not to walk.

> *Let us walk honestly, as in the day; not in rioting and drunkenness, not in chambering and wantonness, not in strife and envying.14 But put ye on the Lord Jesus Christ, and make not provision for the flesh, to fulfil the lusts thereof. (Romans 13:13-14).*

The manifestation of strife was evidence of the carnal condition at the church in Corinth.

> *For it hath been declared unto me of you, my brethren, by them which are of the house of Chloe, that there are contentions among you. (1 Corinthians 1:11).*

> *For ye are yet carnal: for whereas there is among you envying, and strife, and divisions, are ye not carnal, and walk as men? (1 Corinthians 3:3).*

Some Christians who hoped to add to Paul's affliction preached Christ of envy and strife.

Some indeed preach Christ even of envy and strife; and some also of good will. (Philippians 1:15).

Those who turn from the truth of the Scriptures will cause strife and other similar works of the flesh.

He is proud, knowing nothing, but doting about questions and strifes of words, whereof cometh envy, strife, railings, evil surmisings… (1 Timothy 6:4).

But avoid foolish questions, and genealogies, and contentions, and strivings about the law; for they are unprofitable and vain. (Titus 3:9).

The Scripture says that it is impossible to judge a spiritual man.

But he that is spiritual judgeth all things, yet he himself is judged of no man. (1 Corinthians 2:15).

The opposite could be said of a carnal man characterized by strife. Whenever a question is brought to him with which he disagrees, his first response is not, "Is it Biblical?" or "What does the Bible say?" Rather, it is, "I don't hold to that," without the slightest interest in what the Scriptures teach.

EMULATIONS (ζῆλος—*Zelos*)

The old word *emulations* has lost its usage in contemporary English and should be translated *jealousy*. This word can denote that which is good or bad, depending on the context. Ζῆλος is translated *zeal* several times. For example:

> ...*The zeal of thine house hath eaten me up...* (John 2: 17).

> *Epaphras...For I bear him record, that he hath a great zeal for you...* (Colossians 4:12, 13).

Zeal or jealousy is often a good emotion, for a Christian should be ardent to guard the good testimony of his church or the good reputation of his family and friends; but jealousy has its root in the flesh when there is the desire to guard something for fear of *personal* loss. The cause for this type of zeal is selfishness and not true love, which seeks the best for the object or person loved. This type of selfishness is not based upon fact but fear. Many men in the pulpit today, not realizing that a local church is not a business to control, grasp, and destroy any who threaten their place of prominence. This is ζῆλος in human flesh.

WRATH (θυμοί—*Thumoi*)

"I guess it is just my nature to be hot tempered." How often one has heard such a statement as an excuse for flying off the handle? The truth is that it is the sin nature that promotes hot outbursts of anger. Abbott-Smith defines θυμός as "passion," "hot anger," "wrath."[25] Robertson calls it "stirring emotions, then explosions."[26] Vine says, "hot anger, passion."[27]

The emphasis in this word is something quick, of short duration, blazing up and dying down.[28] This word is used in reference to God at least eight times in the book of Revelation. Again, the transient nature of the word is seen in the short duration of battles at the end of the tribulation. God has divine reason and right for wrath and anger, but with man θυμός is a work of the flesh.

STRIFE (ἐριθεῖαι—*Eritheiai*)

Envy, wrath, and strife are a triad of evil that is recorded also in 2 Corinthians 12:20.

> *For I fear, lest, when I come, I shall not find you such as I would, and that I shall be found unto you such as ye would not: lest there be debates, envyings, wraths, strifes, backbitings, whisperings, swellings, tumults…*

Strife (ἐριθεῖαι) appears with envy also in James 3:14 and 16.

> *But if ye have bitter envying and strife in your hearts, glory not, and lie not against the truth…[16] For where envying and strife is, there is confusion and every evil work.*

It also appears and with vainglory in Philippians 2:3.[29] Strife is a constant bedfellow with envy. Strife primarily relates to "ambition, self-seeking."[30]

Vincent, dealing somewhat with the etymology of the word, writes that it is:

> From ἔριθος hired servant. Ἐριθία is, primarily, labor for hire (see Tob. ii. 11), and is applied to those who serve in official positions for hire or for other selfish purposes, and, in order to gain their ends, promote party spirit or faction.[31]

Strife, translated into the idioms of today, could be politics. The maneuvering of individuals into places of prominence and worldly prosperity has left its brand upon many a church, fellowship, and convention. Many starting out to do good have ended up doing very well. James says this type of promotion is soulish and demon-like, which results in confusion and worthless activity (James 3:14-16). The empire builders in Bible-believing circles may find one day that all this will be worthless works.

> *For we must all appear before the judgment seat of Christ; that every one may receive the things done in his body, according to that he hath done, whether it be good or bad. (2 Corinthians 5:10).*

SEDITIONS (διχοστασίαι—*Dichostasia*)

The word διχοστασίαι occurs only one other time in the New Testament, in Romans 16:17,[32] where it is translated *divisions*. Robertson says it is an "old word for 'standings apart,' cleavages."[33]

A brother who exhibits this flesh work is one from whom Christians are called to separate (Romans 16:17). It is a very serious thing to cause division in a local church. It should be noted that the ones who teach contrary to the Scriptures are the ones who cause divisions.

HERESIES (αἱρέσεις—*Haireseis*)

It is difficult on the surface to see the difference between αἱρέσεις and divisions. Depending on the context, this word can either refer to a group of people or a party who holds to an error, or it may refer in general terms to error itself.

In 1 Corinthians 11:19,[34] the word αἱρέσεις refers to an erroneous group in contrast to the *approved ones*. In 2 Peter 2:1,[35] the heresy points to the corrupt and destructive opinions of the false teachers who will secretly invade the churches.

In the context of Galatians 5, it no doubt refers to the fleshly desire to gather a group around an erroneous doctrine and cause divisions in the church. The word διχοστασίαι could be any kind of division caused by the flesh, but αἱρέσεις looks at the carnal desire for or connection with error.

ENVYINGS (φθόνου—*Phthovou*)

…Envy, is the feeling of displeasure produced by witnessing or hearing of the advantage or prosperity of others; this evil sense always attaches to this word….[36]

Envy is a very common work of the flesh and is in very close relation to pride, except that pride finds its source in another enemy—the devil. Pride is thinking oneself *better* than another, but envy is to *desire* what another has or to be in their place of position or privilege. Envy is the plant that produces jealousy. Jealousy is envy brought to completion. This work of the flesh is quite likely the basis for gambling.

MURDERS (φόνοι—*Phonoi*)

The ease with which this word is discarded from the text is shocking indeed.[37] James confirms that murder is a work of the flesh, as he links murder as the result of warring in the inner part of man.

> *From whence come wars and fightings among you? come they not hence, even of your lusts that war in your members?[2] Ye lust, and have not: ye kill, and desire to have, and cannot obtain: ye fight and war, yet ye have not, because ye ask not. (James 4:1, 2).*

The Lord Jesus says in Matthew 15:19 that murder comes out of the heart of man. The emphasis in Scripture is not so much against taking life (Romans 13:4; Acts 25:11[38]), but of the *malicious* taking of a life. The premeditated taking of a life without just cause—this is murder and a work of the flesh.

People often ask, "Can a Christian commit suicide?" The answer is a very definite yes! A Christian out of fellowship cannot control the works of the flesh any better than an unsaved individual, and murder is a flesh work. Today we see serial killing in action. That is because all the works of the flesh are addictive. Serial killers have stated that when they get done killing someone, they actually feel normal for a while. The greatest murderous activity today is the medical abortion industry.

DRUNKENNESS (μέθαι—*Methai*)

One who expressed this work of the flesh wrote:

> I am an alcoholic. I know what it is like to burn with a desire to drink that is so overpowering that family, job, and friends mean nothing...I also know the joy of deliverance from the power of alcohol addiction.[39]

The only ones who will not admit the tragic extent of this work of the flesh are the ones who satisfy this lust.

Drink has taken five million men and women in the United States, taken them as a master takes slaves… and new acquisitions are going on at the rate of 200,000 a year.[40]

Exactly what is drunkenness? Perhaps the most definitive passage is Ephesians 5:18:

And be not drunk with wine, wherein is excess; but be filled with the Spirit.

Being drunk is compared to being filled with the Spirit. The central idea is control. Just as wine controls the unsaved, the Holy Spirit should control the Christian. The work of the flesh is in the desire to be controlled by an outside medium (alcohol, or other drugs), so the conscience (natural inhibitions) can be overcome without embarrassment.

The sin nature does not produce physical addiction to methyl alcohol; rather, it produces the desire to transfer control in order to fulfill other works of the flesh that would not normally be done by a person controlled by his conscience, society, or some other restraint. Some believers today drink wine because they misunderstand the words in Ephesians 5:18. They read the word *excess* and think that they may drink, just not an excessive amount. The Greek word translated *excess* is really the word for *salvation*. The negative alpha on front of the word means that when a person drinks wine or takes other drugs, there are all kinds of unsaved activities.

REVELLINGS (κῶμοι—*Kōmoi*)

Revellings are the continuation of the party that started with μέθαι, until it turned into wild debauchery. Κῶμος is used two other places in Scripture and in surroundings infamously compatible with its nature. Romans 13:13 states:

Let us walk honestly, as in the day; not in rioting and drunkenness, not in chambering and wantonness, not in strife and envying.

Paul is concerned that Christians order the whole manner of their lives in a proper way free from the lusts of the flesh. Here κῶμοι is translated rioting. This is not referring to the current student hobby of rioting in the streets, but rather to the wild activity of drunken brawls. Peter uses this word in 1 Peter 4:3:

...when we walked in lasciviousness, lusts, excess of wine, revellings (κῶμοις), banquetings, and abominable idolatries.

Barclay summarizes:

Komos expresses a lustful excess in physical and sexual pleasure which is offensive to God and to man alike. It may well be that the best translation of it is that of J. W. C. Wand, when he translates it debauchery.[41]

THE LIKE THINGS

If Paul had been borne along further by the Spirit, there could have been a longer list, but he has given enough for anyone to see the trend and nature of the works of the flesh. A literal translation of the like things could be the like things to these. The following is a list of some like things:

1. πάθη ἀτιμίας—passions of dishonor (Romans 1:26)
2. πλεονεξία—covetousness (Romans 1:29)
3. δόλου—guile (Romans 1:29)
4. κακοηθείας—malignity (Romans 1:29)
5. ψιθυριστάς—whisperers (Romans 1:29)
6. καταλάλους—railers (Romans 1:30).
7. θεοστυγείς—God haters (Romans 1:30)
8. ὑβριστάς—insolent (Romans 1:30)
9. ὑπερηθάνους—arrogant (Romans 1:30)
10. γονεῦσιν ἀπειθεῖς—disobedient to parents (Romans 1:30)
11. ἀστόργους—without natural affection (Romans 1:31)
12. ἀνελεήμονας—unmerciful (Romans 1:31)
13. κοίταις—chambering (Romans 13:13)
14. ἀσελγείαις—excesses (Romans 13:13)
15. αἰσχρότης—baseness (Ephesians 5:4)
16. εὐτραπελία—railing (Ephesians 5:4)
17. πλεονέκτης—greedy (Ephesians 5:5)
18. ἐπιθυμίαν κακήν—bad desire (Colossians 1:5)
19. ὀργήν—wrath (Colossians 3:8)

20. κακίαν—malice (Colossians 3:8)
21. θίλαυτοι—self-lovers (2 Timothy 3:2)
22. φιλάργυροι—money-lovers (2 Timothy 3:2)
23. ἀχάριστοι—unthankful (2 Timothy 3:2)
24. ἀνόσιοι—unholy (2 Timothy 3:2)
25. ἀνήμεοι—untamed (2 Timothy 3:3)
26. ἀκρατεῖς—incontinent (2 Timothy 3:3)
27. ἀφιλάγαθοι—haters of good men (2 Timothy 3:3)
28. προπετεῖς—reckless (2 Timothy 3:4)
29. φιλήδονοι—pleasure lovers (2 Timothy 3:4)
30. ἀνόητοι—senseless (Titus 3:3)
31. ἡδοναῖα—pleasures (Titus 3:3)
32. μισοῦντες—hating (Titus 3:3)
33. ἀσελγείαις—licentiousnesses (1 Peter 4:3)
34. οἰνοφλυΐαις—debaucheries (1 Peter 4:3)
35. πότοις—drinking bouts (1 Peter 4:3)
36. ἀθέσμων—loveless (2 Peter 2:7)
37. τολμηταί—darers (2 Peter 2:10)
38. αὐθάδεις—self-satisfied (2 Peter 2:10)
39. ἐντρυφῶντες—reveling (2 Peter 2:13)
40. μεμφίμοιροι—querulous (Jude 16)
41. ἀποδιορίζοντες—making separations (Jude 19)

These works do not present a pretty picture and should not appear in the Christian's life. The absence of such works does not prove a Christian is being controlled by the Holy Spirit, for family and society may be the controlling factor, but the presence of any of these works testifies that he is not Spirit-controlled. Some Christians live most of their lives periodically indulging in certain works of the flesh while thinking the problem is only a bad personality trait. For this reason alone, it is important for believers to understand the activities their sin natures desire to perpetuate. Remember, the works of the flesh are very addictive. A habitual drunkard desires this condition. The fact of addiction explains why some individuals become serial killers. They develop a strong desire to see people die. This is the reason why those in high authority put millions of people to death. They feel great satisfaction in seeing people die.

The Fruit of the Spirit

The activities of the flesh are called works, but the result of the Spirit's ministry is called fruit. The works are individual activities and are in the plural, but the fruit is singular with several segments. It could be compared to an orange—one fruit composed of several sections.

It is important for a Christian to understand these Christian graces, even though he cannot himself produce them. He needs to recognize them and thereby realize the Spirit is controlling him. Also, there is much confusion today as to what these words mean because of erroneous content being poured into them by the unbelieving world. The first segment of the fruit mentioned is love.

LOVE (ἀγάπη—*Agapē*)

But the fruit of the Spirit is love...(Galatians 5:22).

There are about as many definitions of love as there are individuals ready to coin them. Love is a word that is popularly said to defy definition. This idea certainly must come from individuals suffering from an acute case of Biblical illiteracy. The Bible uses the word *love* (ἀγάπη and ἀγαπάω) at least 258 times from the Gospels to the book of Revelation.[42] There is only one book in the New Testament where ἀγάπη or ἀγαπάω does not appear and that, strangely enough, is the book of Acts.[43]

"Agape," said Barclay, "is a word born within the bosom of revealed religion."[44] The word ἀγάπη became filled with new content as the writers of the New Testament used it. This is because ἀγαπάω is of God in this context and is neither displayed through the unsaved nor the carnal Christian (1 John 4:7-12; Galatians 5:22; 1 Corinthians 3:1-3, 13:1-13).

Biblical love has action. God *so loved* that He gave (John 3:16). Not only is there action, but ἀγάπη looks at the motive that produces the action. 1 Corinthians 13:1-13 makes it very clear that it is more important to be properly related to the Holy Spirit than to manifest the Spirit through temporary spiritual gifts. Ἀγάπη can best be defined this way: Love is that segment of the fruit of the Spirit that is the attitude that seeks the will of God for the object loved (Romans 8:28-37; Revelation 12:6, 7). Nothing could be more noble. This type of love is above natural sentimentalism and receives its direction from the Word of God.

And this I pray, that your love may abound yet more and more in knowledge and in all judgment… (Philippians 1:9).

Love not the world, neither the things that are in the world. If any man love the world, the love of the Father is not in him. (1 John 2:15).

JOY (χαρά—*Chara*)

Joy produced by the Holy Spirit is not based on physical circumstances, but rather on the ministry of the third person of the Godhead. To link affliction, joy, and poverty would seem very incongruous to the worldling; however, the Christian is not to be under circumstances, but under grace.

How that in a great trial of affliction the abundance of their joy and their deep poverty abounded unto the riches of their liberality. (2 Corinthians 8:2).

Joy can be caused by happenings, but these are not necessary.

Therefore we were comforted in your comfort: yea, and exceedingly the more joyed we for the joy of Titus, because his spirit was refreshed by you all.
(2 Corinthians 7:13).

This is using the word in similar fashion to the concept of happiness—an attitude relating to or based upon happenings.

Joy is the mental attitude that is absent of sorrow and characterized by a bright, calm, cheerful spirit; in fact, sorrow is contrasted with joy in John 16:20. One other passage links joy with the Holy Spirit:

And ye became followers of us, and of the Lord, having received the word in much affliction, with joy of the Holy Ghost:[7] So that ye were ensamples to all that believe in Macedonia and Achaia. (1 Thessalonians 1:6-7).

The impact of their testimony for the Lord was based upon *the joy of the Holy Ghost*. The ὥστε γενέσθαι proves clearly that the joy of the Lord was a strong magnet that drew others to pattern their lives after the Thessalonian Christians.[45]

It would be difficult to overestimate the power of a joyful testimony. The world knows nothing of this grace. The contrary is also true; the effect of a long-faced Christian's testimony may be far-reaching.

PEACE (εἰρήνη—*Eirēnē*)

The condition of the unsaved is this:

And the way of peace have they not known. (Romans 3:17).

Peace replaces anxiety in the child of God when he is walking in fellowship with the Lord (Philippians 4:6, 7). This peace will garrison the heart and mind of the Christian; the ability of God's peace to do this is beyond contemplation.

The pagan's concept of peace is pictured as a stagnant pond, while the Biblical concept of peace is the boat that is completely controlled on a violent, raging sea.[46] Peace is that unruffled attitude of spirit that transcends outward circumstances. This peace is not what the present generation of worldlings are talking about; they know nothing but lust and war. Christ gives peace that is not of this world (John 14:27). A believing sinner immediately has peace with God (Romans 5:1), for he has believed the *gospel of peace* (Romans 10:15) that came from the *God of peace* (Romans 16:20). Peace as a segment of the fruit of the Spirit is known only to those who have the mind of the Spirit.

For to be carnally minded is death; but to be spiritually minded is life and peace. (Romans 8:6).

Peace is so important that God has told the Christian peace is to rule in his heart.

And let the peace of God rule in your hearts, to the which also ye are called in one body; and be ye thankful. (Colossians 3:15).

LONGSUFFERING (μακροθυμία—*Makrothumia*)

In a day when blowing the stack is encouraged by psychologists as an emotional safety valve, the Spirit-led Christian's answer is the grace of longsuffering. The word μακροθυμία is made up of μαρός, which refers to a long time period, and θυμός, which refers to hot anger.[47] The Christian who exhibits longsuffering can withstand situations in his everyday life that would provoke an unbeliever to outbursts of anger.

God is said to have been longsuffering regarding mankind in the days of Noah (1 Peter 3:2). The wickedness of mankind was great, but God waited. The Lord is never longsuffering with anything but mankind. He speaks to the elements and they obey immediately, but with man He is longsuffering. According to 2 Timothy 4:2,[48] this attitude must accompany the rebuking and exhorting ministry of the Word of God.

GENTLENESS (χρηστότης—*Chrēstotēs*)

A Scottish preacher once said, "If you're not very kind, you're not very holy." A Spirit-filled Christian should be gentle, or—as it might be better translated—kind.

Not every Christian can have the same temperamental traits, as Tim LaHaye points out in his book on Spirit-controlled temperaments; but a Christian can have his old nature controlled, a control evidenced by kindness.[49]

God's kindness is seen in reference to what He has done for lost sinners in His grace. When mankind was guilty of despising His kindness (Romans 2:4),[50] while having no kindness of their own (Romans 3:12),[51] God in His love and kindness (Titus 3:4)[52] sent His Son to save lost sinners. God's kindness is not only seen in saving sinners; in the ages to come, God will exhibit His kindness to the church.

That in the ages to come he might shew the exceeding riches of his grace in his kindness toward us through Christ Jesus. (Ephesians 2:7).

God shows His kindness to sinners yet maintains His righteous standard. The Christian, being controlled by the Spirit, should display this same characteristic.

Kindness is so important that Paul says the Lord's servant should be kind in order that, *the ministry be not blamed* (2 Corinthians 6:3, 6). A Christian is kind when he has a forgiving spirit.

And be ye kind one to another, tenderhearted, forgiving one another, even as God for Christ's sake hath forgiven you. (Ephesians 4:32).

This Christian kindness is a lovely thing, and its loveliness comes from the fact that Christian kindness means treating others in the way in which God has treated us.[53]

GOODNESS (ἀγαθωσύνη—*Agathōsunē*)

The meaning of the Christian grace goodness is rather difficult to define, or at least to distinguish adequately. Ἀγαθωσύνη is used only three times in the Epistles but does not appear in secular Greek.[54] The suffix σύνη was used to coin new words, as is done in English and other languages today. Metzger says that, "The abstract idea of quality is indicated by…-σύνη."[55]

If this idea is true, then the believer who is walking by the Spirit has a quality of goodness about him in reference to manifesting Christ through his life. Goodness is a relative item. For example, a person can be good at baseball, but not at speaking. A Christian's goodness is defined by how he represents his Lord in whatever he is doing. A believer in fellowship with God may not be a good businessman according to the world's standards, but he will be good in his testimony for Christ.

FAITH (πίστις—*Pistis*)

Now faith is the substance of things hoped for, the evidence of things not seen. (Hebrews 11:1).

There are at least three types of faith in the Bible. There is saving faith, which is the gift of God.

For by grace are ye saved through faith; and that not of yourselves: it is the gift of God... (Ephesians 2:8).

There is an attitude of faith by which a Christian is to live; this is a part of the fruit of the Spirit. There is also the *measure of faith* to operate his spiritual gift.

For I say, through the grace given unto me, to every man that is among you, not to think of himself more highly than he ought to think; but to think soberly, according as God hath dealt to every man the measure of faith. (Romans 12:3).

A Christian goes from an act of faith in salvation to an attitude of faith to live the Christian life, for the just are to live by faith.

For therein is the righteousness of God revealed from faith to faith: as it is written, The just shall live by faith. (Romans 1:17).

The word πίστις is very common in the Bible and is used 24 times in Hebrews 11. This same chapter proves that faith is not merely the power of positive thinking. God-given faith is actually a reality of things for which Christians hope. Faith has been the vital approach to God throughout the dispensations; however, the content of things that people have believed changes. Faith as a segment of the Spirit's fruit is the continual attitude of mind that counts as real—what God has given to the believer, whether it be the present position in Christ or future promises of heaven. Faith does not remove the problems that face a child of God from day to day; it provides the link that allows God to overcome the obstacles in the pathway of life.

MEEKNESS (πραΰτης—*Prautēs*)

> *No friend like Him is so high and holy,*
> *No, not one! No, not one!*
> *And yet no friend is so meek and lowly,*
> *No, not one! No, not one!*[56]

The high and holy is coupled in this song with the meek and lowly, for it is Scripturally true that they are not mutually exclusive. There is, however, a popular belief that being meek means to developing a hen-pecked mentality, to lack backbone or determination. This belief, in superficial ways, may appear similar to the idea of meekness; but in fact it is far removed from a true definition. The Bible presents meekness as one's rational and proper control of emotion.

If it is true that you are known by the company you keep, then meekness must be put high on the honor list, for consider the following:

1. "...by the meekness and...gentleness of Christ..." (2 Corinthians 10:1).
2. "...meekness, temperance..." (Galatians 5:23).
3. "...with all lowliness and meekness..." (Ephesians 4:2).
4. "...meekness, longsuffering..." (Colossians 3:12).
5. "...patience, meekness..." (1 Timothy 6:11).

Vine comments on the word πραΰτης as follows, "The meaning of *praütēs* is not readily expressed in English, for the terms meekness, mildness, commonly used, suggest weakness and pusillanimity to a greater or less extent, whereas *praütēs* does nothing of the kind." He states further:

> The common assumption is that when a man is meek it is because he cannot help himself; but the Lord was "meek" because he had the infinite resources of God at His command. Described negatively, meekness is the opposite to self-assertiveness and self-interest; it is equanimity of spirit that is neither elated nor cast down, simply because it is not occupied with self at all.[57]

An interesting use of the word meekness in secular Greek reads:

Prautēs, he goes on to say is the observance of the meaning in relation to anger. The man who is *praus* is the man who feels anger "on the right grounds, and against the right persons, and in the right manner, and at the right moment, and for the right length of time."[58]

In defining the word, it is further stated:

It is when we have *prautēs* that we treat all men with perfect courtesy, that we can rebuke without rancor, that we can argue without intolerance, that we can face the truth without resentment, that we can be angry and yet sin not, that we can be gentle and yet not weak. *Prautēs* is the virtue in which our relationships both with ourselves and our fellowmen become perfect and complete.[59]

Since the root idea of πραΰτης is self-control, it is the segment of the fruit of the Spirit that enables the Christian to control his attitude and actions toward others and use his emotions properly.

TEMPERANCE (ἐγκράτεια—*Enkrateia*)

The word ἐγκράτεια is last in the list, but it should not appear last in the believer's life because his desires must be under the control of the Holy Spirit. Paul reasoned of righteousness and temperance before Felix and Drusilla (Acts 24:25). Considering their "flesh work" relationship, Paul spoke of the lack of self-control.[60]

Wuest says of temperance:

> The word thus refers to the mastery of one's own desires and impulses. The word does not in itself refer to the control of any particular or specific desire or impulse.[61]

Christians today are pressured from many sides—at work, at school, and at home; but each area could be transformed into a place of great testimony for the Lord if the grace of self-control is manifest.

The child of God must have some knowledge of the spiritual walk before he is able to stand against spiritual wickedness in the heavenlies (Ephesians 6:12). The devil and his demons present the next challenge to the Christian. It will help the maturing Christian much if, while enduring temptation, he realizes God is allowing these things to mold him into the image of His Son (Romans 8:29). The works of the flesh and the fruit of the Spirit are important terms for the maturing Christian to understand. The more crucial issue, however, is for the believer to realize he cannot produce the fruit of the Spirit or control the flesh himself.[62] The Christian must learn to order his life by the Spirit, and then when the flesh rises up in an attempt to control the individual, the Spirit of God will oppose the sin principle so the works of the flesh will not appear.

Endnotes

1. Romans 7 is speaking of the saved, not the unsaved, as Romans 7:22 points out.
2. Beirne Lay, Jr., "Upward!," *Reader's Digest* (March, 1958), p. 224.
3. *Wherefore, as by one man sin entered into the world, and death by sin; and so death passed upon all men, for that all have sinned... (Romans 5:12).*
4. *That as sin hath reigned unto death, even so might grace reign through righteousness unto eternal life by Jesus Christ our Lord. (Romans 5:21).*
5. William Barclay, *Flesh and Spirit* (Nashville, Tenn.: Abingdon Press, 1962), p. 10.
6. Lewis Sperry Chafer, *He That Is Spiritual* (3rd ed.; Grand Rapids: Dunham Publishing Co., 1966), p. 151.
7. *Who opposeth and exalteth himself above all that is called God, or that is worshipped; so that he as God sitteth in the temple of God, shewing himself that he is God. (2 Thessalonians 2:4).*
8. Kenneth S. Wuest, *Galatians in the Greek New Testament* (Grand Rapids: Wm. B. Eerdmans Publishing Co., 1944), p. 153.
9. *This I say then, walk in the Spirit, and ye shall not fulfil the lust of the flesh.[17] For the flesh lusteth against the Spirit, and the Spirit against the flesh: and these are contrary the one to the other: so that ye cannot do the things that ye would. (Galatians 5:16-17).*
10. W.F. Arndt and F. Wilbur Gingrich, *A Greek-English Lexicon of the New Testament and Other Early Christian Literature* (Chicago: The University of Chicago Press, 1957), p. 655.

11 W.E. Vine, *An Expository Dictionary of New Testament Words*, IV (Old Tappan, New Jersey: Fleming H. Revell Co., 1940), 195.
12 Wuest, *Galatians*, p. 153.
13 Chafer, *He That*, p. 120.
14 Tim LaHaye, *Spirit-Controlled Temperament* (Wheaton, Illinois: Tyndale House Publishers, 1966), p. 80.
15 G. Abbott-Smith, *A Manual Greek Lexicon of the New Testament* (Edinburgh: T. & T. Clark, 1921), p. 161.
16 G.K. Gillespie, *The Englishman's Greek Concordance of the New Testament* (London: Samuel Bagster & Sons, Ltd., 1903), p. 465.
17 J.B. Lightfoot, *The Epistle of St. Paul to the Galatians* (Grand Rapids: Zondervan Publishing House, 1957), p. 210.
18 Barclay, *Flesh*, p. 39.
19 Gerhard Kittel (ed.), *Theological Dictionary of the New Testament*, IV (Grand Rapids: Wm. B. Eerdmans Publishing Co., 1967), p. 732.
20 Barclay, *Flesh*, p. 25.
21 James Hope Moulton and George Milligan, *The Vocabulary of the Greek Testament* (Grand Rapids: Wm. B. Eerdmans Publishing Co., 1963), p. 16.
22 Arndt and Gingrich, *A Greek-English*, p. 114.
23 Lightfoot, *The Epistle*, p. 210.
24 Barclay, *Flesh*, pp. 32-33.
25 Abbott-Smith, *A Manual*, p. 210.
26 A.T. Robertson, *Word Pictures in the New Testament*, IV (Nashville: Broadman Press, 1931), p. 312.
27 Vine, *An Expository*, 239.
28 Barclay, *Flesh*, p. 52.

29 *Let nothing be done through strife or vainglory; but in lowliness of mind let each esteem other better than themselves. (Philippians 2:3).*
30 Abbott-Smith, A *Manual*, p. 179.
31 Marvin R. Vincent, *Word Studies in the New Testament*, IV (Grand Rapids: Wm. B. Eerdmans Publishing Co., 1946), p. 165.
32 *Now I beseech you, brethren, mark them which cause divisions and offences contrary to the doctrine which ye have learned; and avoid them. (Romans 16:17).*
33 Robertson, *Word*, IV, p. 428.
34 *For there must be also heresies among you, that they which are approved may be made manifest among you. (1 Corinthians 11:19).*
35 *But there were false prophets also among the people, even as there shall be false teachers among you, who privily shall bring in damnable heresies, even denying the Lord that bought them, and bring upon themselves swift destruction. (2 Peter 2:1).*
36 Vine, *An Expository*, II, 37.
37 Most who hold the Westcott and Hart text omit this word, even though the word is found in MSS A, D, G, and the majority of MSS representing the "Majority-text." The omission of the word can easily be explained by haplography, ΦΘΟΝΟΙΦΟΝΟΙ, by failing to repeat letters that occur twice.
38 *For if I be an offender, or have committed any thing worthy of death, I refuse not to die: but if there be none of these things whereof these accuse me, no man may deliver me unto them. I appeal unto Caesar. (Acts 25:11).*

39 Jerry G. Dunn, *God is for the Alcoholic* (Chicago: Moody Press, 1965), jacket.
40 S.I. McMillen, *None of These Diseases* (Westwood, New Jersey: Fleming H. Revell Co., 1963), p. 25.
41 Barclay, *Flesh*, p. 62.
42 J.B. Smith, *Greek-English Concordance to the New Testament* (Scottdale, Pennsylvania: Herald Press, 1955), p. 2.
43 There are several other words used for *love* in the New Testament. For studies on these, students should read Kenneth S. Wuest's *Bypaths in the Greek New Testament* (Grand Rapids: Wm. B. Eerdmans Publishing Co., 1940), pp. 109-21.
44 Barclay, *Flesh*, p. 64.
45 A.T. Robertson, *A Grammar of the Greek New Testament in the Light of Historical Research* (Nashville: Broadman Press, 1934), p. 1000.
46 Barclay, *Flesh*, p. 84.
47 Moulton and Milligan, *The Vocabulary*, p. 386.
48 *Preach the word; be instant in season, out of season; reprove, rebuke, exhort with all longsuffering and doctrine. (2 Timothy 4:2).*
49 LaHaye, *Spirit-Controlled*, p. 8. His emphasis is good on the types of temperaments, but he is in error at one point because he says temperaments can be changed and then equates temperaments with the old nature.
50 *Or despisest thou the riches of his goodness and forbearance and longsuffering; not knowing that the goodness of God leadeth thee to repentance? (Romans 2:4).*
51 *They are all gone out of the way, they are together become unprofitable; there is none that doeth good, no, not one. (Romans 3:12).*

52 *But after that the kindness and love of God our Savior toward man appeared. (Titus 3:4).*
53 Barclay, *Flesh*, p. 102.
54 Moulton and Milligan, *The Vocabulary*, p. 1.
55 Bruce M. Metzger, *Lexical Aids for Students of New Testament Greek* (Princeton, New Jersey: By the author, 1965), p. 56.
56 Johnson Oatman, "No Not One," in *Inspiring Hymns*, compiled by Alfred B. Smith (Grand Rapids: Singspiration, Inc., 1951), Hymn No. 435.
57 Vine, *An Expository*, III, 56.
58 Barclay, *Flesh*, p. 120.
59 Ibid., p. 121.
60 F.F. Bruce, *The Book of the Acts* (Grand Rapids: Wm. B. Eerdmans Publishing Co., 1954), p. 472.
61 Wuest, *Galatians*, p. 160.
62 Please refer to the discussion of the control of the flesh on page 26.

CHAPTER 2

THE CHRISTIAN'S DEFENSE AGAINST THE DEVIL

That there is a Devil is a thing doubted by none but such as are under the influences of the Devil. For any to deny the being of a Devil must be from an ignorance of profaneness worse than diabolical.

Cotton Mather

No individual can be victorious against the adversary of our souls unless he understands that adversary—unless he understands his philosophy, his methods of operation, and his methods of temptation. We hear very little today about Satan, and consequently many who recognize Satan's existence and acknowledge he is the enemy of their souls are ill-prepared to meet him.[1]

When a Christian realizes how the Holy Spirit opposes the sin nature, he will be prepared to understand how Satan works to remove him from fellowship with the Lord to sinful independence.

The Motive of the Devil

Before it is possible to understand Satan's temptations and their purpose, it is mandatory to understand and appreciate his motive. According to the Scriptures, the supreme motive of Satan is his purpose to become like the Most High. Though that purpose was formed even before the age of man, it has been his constant actuating motive from that time until now.[2]

In fact, some kind of evolution is absolutely necessary for those who would reject God. Thus, the idea of an evolutionary origin must have had its first beginnings in the mind of Satan himself, as the only means by which he could rationalize his rebellion against God. The only evidence he had that he was actually a creature of God was the fact that God said so. If he rejected the Word of God, then he must assume that he, along with other beings in the universe and with the non-living components of the universe, and even God Himself, had somehow evolved by innate processes of an eternally existing universe into their present state. Thus, God's rule may simply have been a coincidence of priority of time of evolution and might be overcome by a well-planned and executed rebellion.[3]

Satan was the anointed cherub before unrighteousness was found in him (Ezekiel 28).[4] Note the words of Isaiah concerning Lucifer:

How art thou fallen from heaven, O Lucifer, son of the morning! how art thou cut down to the ground, which didst weaken the nations! [13] *For thou hast said in thine heart, I will ascend into heaven, I will exalt my throne above the stars of God: I will sit also upon the mount of the congregation, in the sides of the north:*[14] *I will ascend above the heights of the clouds; I will be like the most High. (Isaiah 14:12-14).*

It should be clearly understood that when Satan said he would be like the Most High, he was not desiring to be holy, just, and righteous, which might be reckoned a noble ambition. On the contrary, he wanted to be like God in only one respect: He wanted to be independent and worshipped like God. Henry Morris points out that perhaps it was the idea of evolution that prompted the anointed cherub to think he could get by with such a bold venture.

Satan's motive is seen in the purpose of his temptations, for he desires to have men follow him in his quest for complete independence from the rule of God.

The Temptations of the Devil

In order for the devil to fulfill his motive, he planned well how to capture the thoughts and actions of the humans who came to live in Eden. To meet the demands of his supreme motive, he became the master counterfeiter, the father of lies, the one who deceives the nations (2 Corinthians 11:14; John 8:44; Revelation 12:9, 20:2, 3, 7, 8). These characteristics set the nature of his temptations.

THE NATURE OF THE TEMPTATIONS

The popular concept of Satan's temptations could be summed up in the erroneous statement attributed to John Wesley: "All the works of our evil nature are the work of the devil."[5] S.I. McMillen—in his valuable and interesting book, *None of These Diseases*—also confuses the enemies when he writes, "These people have the devil to pay because they paid no attention to God's Word: 'Neither let us commit fornication, as some of them committed, and fell in one day three and twenty thousand.'"[6]

The Bible, however, states in Galatians 5:19:

Now the works of the flesh are manifest, which are these; Adultery, fornication...

Even books that deal with Satan's temptation, such as worry, do not really deal with the enemy, but rather go directly to the defense.[7] The nature of the devil's temptations must be clearly understood so a proper appreciation of the nature of the defense can be made and the armor applied.

Satan does not have to make approaches through the sin nature of the Christian or through the world's system. This fact comes into clear focus in observing how Satan tempted Eve and then Adam.

Before the fall, there was no flesh in the sense of Galatians 5 or Romans 7. There was no κόσμος system at that time. Therefore, the devil came directly to Eve and placed an idea in her mind to weigh and consider. Satan immediately questioned the Word of God:

Ye shall not surely die… (Genesis 3:4b).

Note that he did not suggest to her she should doubt the Word. He suggests that if she would just eat of the tree, she would be like God. She would know what was good for her and what was bad.

As it has been shown, "This was the first commencement address, 'Go out and make something of yourself.'" Satan's words are found in verse five, but Satan's thoughts are found in verse six. The tree was *good for food*. (After all, Adam needed more variety in his diet.) The tree was *pleasant to the eyes*. (Adam would think highly of her for her well-developed esthetic nature.) The tree was *desired to make one wise*. (Adam would not want her to be a dumb blonde.) What could possibly be wrong with such noble thoughts? Only one thing: They would produce an action contrary to the stated Word of God.

Neither Adam nor Eve had a sin nature to which Satan could appeal. Similarly, when Satan tempted Christ, he could make no solicitation to a flesh nature, for Christ had none.

For we have not an high priest which cannot be touched with the feeling of our infirmities; but was in all points tempted like as we are, yet without sin. (Hebrews 4:15).

The fact is that Christ was tempted (πειρασθῆναι, Matthew 4:1) to evil. Satan does not make his appeal to the sin nature for at least three reasons: First, the strong desires of the flesh are under control for the Spirit-filled Christian;[8] second, Satan's purpose is not to get men to be controlled completely by the flesh works; third, he can go directly to the mind and heart with his thoughts, which do not come close to approximating the lusts of the flesh.

The Scriptures reveal at least three approaches the devil uses to accomplish his purposes with Christians. They appear under the terminology *wiles*, *devices*, and *snares*.

The wiles of the devil

Put on the whole armor of God, that ye may be able to stand against the wiles of the devil. (Ephesians 6:11).

The Greek word for *wiles* is μεθοδείας. It is used one other time in the Epistles, in Ephesians 4:14,[9] where it is translated by the King James Version as *lie in wait*. The idea of wiles seems to be a method or approach of craftiness in tempting believers. Robertson says:

> *Methodia* is from *methodeuō* (*meta, hodos*) to follow after or up, to practice deceit, and occurs nowhere else (Ephesians 4:13; 6:11) save in late papyri in the sense of method. The word *planēs* (wandering like our "planet") adds to the evil idea in the word.[10]

Vine concurs by saying μεθοδείας, "denotes craft, deceit...a cunning device...."[11] The context of Ephesians 6:10-17 is the use of the armor as defense against the devious strategies of the devil. The term *wiles of the devil* emphasizes the deceitful methodology of his temptations. Satanic temptations never appear on the surface as they really are. This idea no doubt accounts for the repeated warning for Christians to be sober and watchful in reference to Satanic temptations (1 Peter 4:7, 5:8; 2 Timothy 1:7, 2:24-26; Titus 2:4, 6).

The devices of the devil

The devices of Satan relate to the form his temptations take. The word *device* is found in 2 Corinthians 2:11:

> *Lest Satan should get an advantage of us: for we are not ignorant of his devices.*

The context deals with the man who had been disciplined by the church because of Paul's admonishment in 1 Corinthians

5:1-8. This man had apparently repented of his immorality, confessed his sin, and was now in fellowship with God. The church was to forgive him; not to forgive would be giving way to a thought (device) of the devil.

The word νοήματα is used five other times in the Epistles. In 2 Corinthians 3:14, 4:4, 11:3 and Philippians 4:7, it is translated *minds*; it is translated *thought* in 2 Corinthians 10:5. Thus, the concept or thought rising in the minds of some was an unforgiving spirit. The emphasis in the word *devices*, as used in 2 Corinthians 2:11[12] is that Satanic temptations are mental attitudes or thoughts. The devil apparently has the ability to put his thoughts in the hearts of Christians when allowed by God. An example of this is seen in the account of Ananias and Sapphira in Acts 5:

...why hath Satan filled thine heart to lie... (Acts 5:3).

It should be noted that there is no sin involved by the entrance of these thoughts; it is what a believer does with these thoughts that determines whether sin will enter and break fellowship with the Lord.

The snare of the devil

Perhaps one of the most common phenomena in this era of Biblical illiteracy is Satanic ensnarement. There is only one passage in the Church writings that defines ensnarement:

And the servant of the Lord must not strive; but be gentle unto all men, apt to teach, patient, In meekness instructing those that oppose themselves;[25] if God peradventure will give them repentance to the acknowledging of the truth;[26] And that they may recover themselves out of the snare of the devil, who are taken captive by him at his will. (2 Timothy 2:24-26).

The emphasis in these verses concerns the approach a servant of the Lord must have to a believer who is opposing (literally, it is *the ones opposing, τοὺς ἀντιδιατιθεμένους*); from the same verse, it is obvious they are standing against the truth. This condition is said to be *the snare of the devil*. The ensnared saint is one who, for some reason perhaps unknown to himself, opposes some truth of the Word of God. The ultimate reason they oppose the truth is the fact that Satan has led them astray. Vine comments on the word for *take captive*.

> ZŌGREŌ (ζωγρέω) lit. signifies to take men alive (from *zoōs*, alive, and *agreuō*, to hunt or catch), Luke 5:10 (marg. "take alive"), there of the effects of the work of the Gospel; in 2 Timothy 2:26 it is said of the power of Satan to lead men astray. The verse should read "and that they may recover themselves out of the snare of the Devil (having been taken captive by him), unto the will of God." This is the probable meaning rather than to take alive or for life.[13]

What did Satan do to capture these Christians? The key is found in the words *they may recover themselves*. The word is ἀνανήθω means *to return to soberness*.[14] The word νήφω is used in 1 Peter 5:8:

Be sober, be vigilant; because your adversary the devil, as a roaring lion, walketh about, seeking whom he may devour.

Wuest, commenting on the word sober, says, "In the words 'be sober' sobriety of mind is enjoined. 'Be mentally self-controlled,' is the idea."[15] The idea of thoughts, mind, and mental attitudes again comes to the forefront. Ensnarement, then, is no one specific temptation but could involve different Satanic temptations. The specific practical result in this case is opposition to the truth of the Word of God. Scripture indicates that if an overseer (bishop) has a bad testimony before the unsaved, he will fall into a snare of the devil.

Moreover he must have a good report of them which are without; lest he fall into reproach and the snare of the devil. (1 Timothy 3:7).

Some spiritual leaders fall into the snare of opposing some truth of God's Word in order to justify their unscriptural actions before the world. Satan is after the minds of Christians.

A present-day example is the new false teaching that the Rapture (catching away of the Church, the Body of

Christ) takes place toward the end of the tribulation. This false teaching is called the Pre-Wrath Rapture. The people who hold to this doctrine need to repent and acknowledge the truth that the Dispensation of Grace cannot be mixed up with the Dispensation of Law, as the tribulation period is Daniel's seventy weeks and under the Mosaic Law.

The devil's distractions are subtle, powerful, and never appear on the surface as temptations. In order to achieve his unholy purpose in temptation, the devil's planted thoughts must be masked in a very deceptive way.

THE PURPOSE OF THE TEMPTATIONS

Satan's sin in the beginning was a result of his pride. As stated in Ezekiel 28:17:

Thine heart was lifted up because of thy beauty, thou hast corrupted thy wisdom by reason of thy brightness....

Isaiah 14:13, 14 declares that he said in his heart:

I will ascend into heaven, I will exalt my throne above the stars of God: I will sit upon the mount of the congregation, in the sides of the north: I will ascend above the heights of the clouds; I will be like the most High.

1 Timothy 3:6 cautions concerning a bishop (an overseer):

Not a novice, lest being lifted up with pride he fall into the condemnation of the devil.

When man was created, Satan suggested to Eve to act independently of God. Then through Eve he was able to get Adam to go against God's command. When the devil tempted Christ, each temptation was geared toward getting the Son to act independently of the Father. The main purpose Satan has in tempting believers is to draw them away from walking by the Spirit—to be independent. Basically, this is a form of pride that underlies all of Satan's temptations to evil. This will be mentioned further under each attack. While it is true that pride is basic to each attack, the practical outworking of each is different; the Christian, therefore, needs more than one piece of armor, as mentioned in Ephesians 6.

THE IDENTIFICATION OF THE TEMPTATIONS

There are several key points in this book that are necessary for it to serve a useful, practical purpose. This section must hold a prominent place among them. It should be clear that one cannot defend himself if he does not know he is being tempted—or if, as is so common, he is confused as to the source of the temptation. Though Barnhouse's analysis of the enemies is not Scripturally clear, he does make a point when he says:

> The flesh, the world, and the devil are just as different in their modes of attack as are the varied branches of

service in earthly warfare. The success of our defense will depend upon our understanding of the differences between the three and the use of the divinely appointed methods of their defeat.[16]

The importance of singling out the enemy and isolating the temptation no doubt accounts for the warnings in Scripture to be sober and vigilant (1 Peter 5:8). The Scriptures identify Satan's devices for the believer in very clear language.

Pride

Pride, while foundational to all of Satan's temptations, must be treated separately because Scripture indicates it is a single wile in itself.

The word τυφωθείς in 1 Timothy 3:6 is translated *pride*. It comes from τυφοω, which in common words means *smoke*.[17] The idea is metaphorical in the sense that this novice or newly planted one is like smoke rising higher and higher in his own estimation—or, in the Authorized Version phraseology, *being lifted up*. The same word is used in 1 Timothy 6:4, translated *proud*, and 2 Timothy 3:4, translated *high-minded*. The devil is linked directly to this temptation. Boasting in the bad sense has pride as its source.

Age conforming or independence from God

Closely related to pride and the purpose of Satan's temptations is a disposition of mind to act independently of God. The actual terminology refers to believers who are abiding in

Christ while slowly directing their love toward this present evil age. The Scriptures reveal that believers now live not only in the Dispensation of Grace, but also in this evil age.

First of all, an age is a period of time where some special things are happening, and it differs from a dispensation. You sometimes hear people talk about the Age of Grace. There is no such phrase in the Bible. The age mentioned here is a time where there is much evil because Satan is the god of this age (2 Corinthians 4:4).[18] The evilness is seen in the fact that whatever Satan does is done independently of the Holy One.

Demas, at one time a fellow laborer of Paul (Philem. 24), is an example of one who so succumbed. Thus in 2 Timothy 4:10 Paul laments:

> *For Demas hath forsaken me, having loved this present world [the Greek is the word for age] and is departed unto Thessalonica....*

Demas was acting independently of God and drifting because he loved the evil age. He showed his love and conformation to the age by concurring in the thought of independence planted in his mind and heart. The believers in Rome were exhorted to stop being conformed (as the present imperative συσχηματίζεσθε indicates) to this age.

> *I beseech you therefore, brethren, by the mercies of God, that ye present your bodies a living sacrifice, holy, acceptable unto God, which is your reasonable service.*[2] *And be*

not conformed to this world: but be ye transformed by the renewing of your mind, that ye may prove what is that good, and acceptable, and perfect, will of God. (Romans 12:1-2).

This act of independence in Romans 12 is related to Christian service. They were to realize that not only were they saved by grace (Romans 4:4)[19] and to live by grace (Romans 7:25),[20] they were to serve the Lord the same way by using their renewed mind. That is, they were to allow the Holy Spirit to manifest Himself through them for true spiritual service, for every Christian has a gift for service. Scripture states:

But the manifestation of the Spirit is given to every man to profit withal… (1 Corinthians 12:7).

Romans 12:3-6[21] confirms that anyone who goes about the Lord's work with an air of self-sufficiency thinks of himself more highly than he ought and does not think soberly to be put in a place of usefulness. This temptation is as common today as the cough of a cold, but with more frightful complications. There are few in Bible-believing fundamental circles who will tolerate, much less encourage, their church to function on the basis of the permanent spiritual gifts.

Worry

We were shocked during World War II at the news that one-third of a million of our finest young people were killed in combat. The fact that during the same period over a million civilians died from heart disease—much of it caused by worry—provoked hardly the raising of an eyebrow.[22]

Peter says:

Casting all your care upon him: for he careth for you.
(1 Peter 5:7).

Verse eight is often ignored when the promise in verse seven is pleaded:

Be sober, be vigilant; because your adversary the devil, as a roaring lion, walketh about, seeking whom he may devour.
(1 Peter 5:8).

Satan is tied closely to the problem of the Christian's anxiety. The saints to whom Peter was writing were in danger of anxiety because of a temptation to be proud. Notice verse six:

Humble yourselves therefore under the mighty hand of God, that he may exalt you in due time.

This pride came in the form of self-pity because they were undergoing afflictions at the time. Whether the afflictions were caused by Satan is irrelevant at this point. The greatest emergency was within their own hearts. Apparently, the roaring lion had placed in their minds that they were too good, too valuable, too important in God's service to undergo such afflictions. This subtle form of pride will put one in a mental state called worry.

What is the Christian's main problem regarding worry? Is it not true that the real problem in the crucible of life is the ability and knowledge to cast our cares upon the Lord, and then—perhaps even more difficult—leave them there? It is not difficult to leave the burdens there if one knows the enemy who is causing him to worry and the subsequent defense. The secret of having victory over worry is proper use of the Scriptural defense God has given us and not the power of positive thinking.

Discouragement

There is a popular fable that Satan was going out of business and having a garage sale so he could get rid all his tools of temptation. Most of the insidious tools were reasonably priced, but the tool of discouragement was priced much higher than all the rest. When asked why the tool of discouragement was priced so high, he replied, "Because when all the other tools are ineffective, I can usually use discouragement to reach the heart of any Christian and very, very few realize the tool belongs to me."

It is fable that Satan is going out of business, but how tragically true is his evaluation of the use of discouragement. Paul perhaps was tempted to be discouraged when he desired to see the Thessalonian Christians but was not allowed to by Satan.

But we, brethren, being taken from you for a short time in presence, not in heart, endeavored the more abundantly to see your face with great desire.[18] Wherefore we would have come unto you, even I Paul, once and again; but Satan hindered us. (1 Thessalonians 2:17-18).

Paul's desire was to see the Thessalonian Christians, and twice he made an effort to go to them, but Satan would not allow it. Being once hindered in satisfying a legitimate desire produces disappointment; twice hindered surely multiplies the temptation toward discouragement.

Job is the classic illustration of discouragement.

Why died I not from the womb? Why did I not give up the ghost when I came out of the belly? (Job 3:11).

Job was a disappointed man, yet:

In all this Job sinned not, nor charged God foolishly. (Job 1:22).

Perhaps one of the reasons for the book of Job is to reveal to believers today the source of Job's discouragement—Satan. The interesting thing about this particular temptation is that Satan never came directly to Job. Rather, in a more subtle way he brought calamity into Job's life. What would Job do with the apparent tragedy about him? The thought planted by Satan is immediately one of self-pity, which is a form of pride.

Will this device of Satan be nurtured to the point of sin, or will the proper defense be used? Job, while living probably in the dispensation of promise, never had the same panoply of defense the Christian has. Still, he came through victorious.

Let it be repeated again—the devil's temptations never appear to be temptations on the surface; therefore, sober-mindedness is enjoined.

Cowardice in spiritual things

Even the bravest of men feels a moment of fear when a spiritual opportunity arrives. The Christian is tempted because of fear and then fails to follow the Spirit's leading. Peter boasted that he would follow the Lord, even to death if necessary (John 13:37).[23] But when the Lord Jesus was taken it states:

And Peter followed afar off. (Luke 22:54).

Later, while warming himself by the fire, Peter was recognized by a young maid. Peter denied he knew Christ (Luke 22:57). Peter was under the attack of Satan.

And the Lord said, Simon, Simon. behold. Satan hath desired to have you, that he may sift you as wheat;[32] But I have prayed for thee, that thy faith fail not: and when thou art converted. strengthen thy brethren. (Luke 22:31-32).

This proclamation by the Lord Jesus Christ is saturated with meaning and has extensive implications. It is evident from this statement that Satan must request permission from the Lord before he is allowed to tempt a believer. Notice the text again:

Satan hath desired to have you...

Normally, the word translated *desire* would be θελω, indicating something of a wish. Here the word is ἐζητήσατο, which means to earnestly beg. The middle voice carries the idea that Satan earnestly begged for himself to have Peter. The word ἐζαιτέω also has the concept of procurement, indicating again that this is the only way Satan can get at those who are believers.[24]

Satan wanted to sift Peter as grain. The temptation of the great roaring lion came first in the form of a maidservant of the high priest, when she accused Peter of being with Christ (Mark 14:66, 67). The depths of the pond of subtlety is where the old serpent surely must drink.

Timothy was apparently tempted to be cowardly, for Paul wrote:

For God hath not given us the spirit of fear; but of power, and of love, and of a sound mind.[8] Be not thou therefore ashamed of the testimony of our Lord, nor of me his prisoner: but be thou partaker of the afflictions of the gospel according to the power of God...(2 Timothy 1:7-8).

The word *fear* is literally *cowardice*. Timothy was perhaps tempted to be cowardly because of what happened to Paul, who was now a prisoner of Rome. Paul reminded Timothy that this cowardice did not come from the Holy Spirit; rather, God produced power, love, and self-control.

Those who are submissive to the Spirit's control find there is power (*dunameōs*) sufficient to defeat the Evil One, to win others, and to do all that God expects.[25]

It is beyond the scope of this book to relate the spiritual gift mentioned in verse six regarding Timothy's cowardice in being a witness for the Lord. There is some indication that the gift Timothy received to make full proof of his ministry was the gift of evangelism. (Compare 2 Timothy 1:6-8, 2 Timothy 4:5, and 1 Timothy 4:14.)

The temptation to be cowardly is closely related to pride because it only occurs as one contemplates the uncertain consequences that he fears. Pride will not tolerate an uncertain end. Pride and cowardice cannot coexist with an attitude of faith.

Stealing

Some temptations are hard to catalog. Stealing is among these. Ephesians 4:27-28 says:

> *Neither give place to the devil. Let him that stole steal no more: but rather let him labor, working with his hands the thing which is good, that he may have to give to him that needeth.*

There is a definite break between verses 26 and 27, by the word μηδέ (nor). However, the one stealing seems to be closely related to the word *devil*. The word *give* is a present imperative and carries the idea that there were some in the church who were presently giving place to the devil and that they should stop it. The same idea is seen in the next verse with the one who was stealing. Being a thief is certainly one of Satan's marks of notoriety.

Those by the way side are they that hear; then cometh the devil, and taketh away the word out of their hearts, lest they should believe and be saved. (Luke 8:12).

Lying

"*...Ye shall not surely die*" *(Genesis 3:4)* is the first recorded lie of Satan. The devil was a:

...murderer from the beginning, and abode not in the truth, because there is no truth in him. When he speaketh a lie, he speaketh of his own: for he is a liar, and the father of it. (John 8: 44).

The devil is the one who deceives the nations in Revelation 20:8, 10.

And shall go out to deceive the nations which are in the four quarters of the earth, Gog and Magog, to gather them together to battle: the number of whom is as the sand of the sea. (Revelation 20:8).

And the devil that deceived them was cast into the lake of fire and brimstone, where the beast and the false prophet are, and shall be tormented day and night for ever and ever. (Revelation 20:10).

This wicked vice is so much a part of his nature that he desires to plant it in the hearts of God's people.

The prime example of this temptation is found in Acts 5:1-10. Ananias and Sapphira, his wife, sold some of their property to help the Christians in Jerusalem in this time of persecution. According to Acts 2:45, it had been the custom to bring the full selling price of the real estate to the apostles. Apparently, Ananias tried to make Peter think he had given all when he kept back part. To this lie, Peter issued a piercing question: *"...why hath Satan filled thine heart to lie to the Holy Ghost...."*

The consequences were most severe, and Ananias never had much time for remorse. Peter asked a very strange question. Notice he did not say, "Ananias, why did you tell a lie?" Rather, he expressed shock that Ananias allowed Satan to control his heart: *"...why hath Satan filled thine heart to lie...."* Verse four is literally, *"...why hast thou conceived this thing in thine heart? thou has not lied unto men, but unto God."*

The progression of this temptation is interesting. First, Satan began to control the heart. This is the point where Ananias should have resisted. It is history that he did not. *Conceived* in verse four is from ἔθου, an aorist middle of τίθημι, which means to *place, fix,* or *resolve upon it.*[26] Satan controlled the thoughts in his heart to deceive the Holy Spirit, but Ananias determined to act upon this temptation. This accords with James' description. of how sin develops (James 1:13-15).

Laziness in spiritual things

"The devil uses idle hands," is an old saying. Just as true is the statement, "The devil tempts to idleness." The Word of God links idleness to Satanic suggestion.

> *And withal they learn to be idle, wandering about from house to house; and not only idle, but tattlers also and busybodies, speaking things which they ought not.*[14] *I will therefore that the younger women marry, bear children, guide the house, give none occasion to the adversary to speak reproachfully.*[15] *For some are already turned aside after Satan. (1 Timothy 5:13-15).*

The word *idle* (ἀργαὶ), according to Robertson, is from *ergon* (work) and is negated by the α privative.[27] These widows apparently felt no need to be home workers—as Titus 2:5 commands for married women—but felt free to travel from house to house or, literally *wander around the houses.* This could mean they were going from church to church, since most of the churches at that time met in homes. This particular type of wandering never ends in itself, but its natural outcome is gossiping.

Tale bearing

The popular concept of Christian fellowship sometimes degenerates into nothing more than coffee, doughnuts, and gossip. Gossip or tattling is listed along with idleness in 1 Timothy 5:11-15[28] as having its source with Satan. The devil, who is the accuser of the brethren, promotes others to do his work here on earth.

The word *tattlers* means, "to boil up, to throw up bubbles, like blowing soap bubbles."[29] Just as soap bubbles have little content, so does the gossip. Their words mean "nonsense, talk idly, prate, to bring forward idle accusations, make empty charges, to accuse one falsely with malicious words."[30]

In this passage, the gossips are women, but this temptation is not limited to the so-called weaker sex. People who talk down about other people soon run out of things to say. It becomes necessary to hunt up new dirt, which requires them to develop into busybodies.

Busybody

A busybody is one who takes great pains to pry into the affairs of others. This delicate art no doubt is sometimes done under the pious mask of being able to pray more intelligently. The term translated *busybody* in 1 Timothy 5:13 is περίεργοι. The neuter form is used in Acts 19:19 and is translated *curious arts*. Those taken up with curious arts are interested in prying into things and telling the future.

The busybody works, but not at his own business (2 Thessalonians 3:11).[31] He looks into the affairs of others for dirt. Upon finding it, he uses his tongue as a trowel to spread it.

An unforgiving spirit

It is very difficult to remove the scars of sin. Perhaps because of this fact, Christians find it difficult to forgive as they should. To maintain an unforgiving attitude when the sinning party has confessed his sin is to follow one of Satan's devices. Second Corinthians 2:10, 11 states:

To whom ye forgive anything, I forgive also: for if I forgave any thing, to whom I forgave it, for your sakes forgave I it in the person of Christ;[11] Lest Satan should get an advantage of us: for we are not ignorant of his devices.

Everyone has a strong natural tendency to hold grudges. This tendency possibly stems from the concept that one should pay fully for what he has done. The Scriptural attitude, however, is one of forgiveness. Ephesians 4:32 says:

And be ye kind one to another, tenderhearted, forgiving one another, even as God for Christ's sake hath forgiven you.

Once a Christian has discovered the source of temptation, he is now ready to apply the proper defense. He must not only understand the nature of the temptation, but also the nature of the defense before he can use it with any measure of success. No doubt many Christians have unknowingly made use of the armor of God, but this ignorant approach is exceedingly slow—at best a trial-and-error method. It is far better if the Christian intelligently understands his spiritual patterns for maturity.

The Defenses for Satanic Temptations

Misunderstanding and misuse have been the long and dismal history of the defenses against Satanic temptations. The defenses against this mighty spirit being have been, for the most part, handled in a piously superstitious fashion. Who is not unfortunately familiar with the following formula: "The devil trembles when he sees the weakest saint upon his knees."[32] Nowhere in the Bible does it say such a thing. The devil is not afraid of any Christian, no matter what he does or says (1 Peter 5:8).

Consider the following:

> We believe the main source of our heartaches for the past few months is Satanic! We believe the reason no souls have been saved recently is due to an all-out attack on our church by the devil! We close our report with a strong recommendation that the congregation call a special meeting, rebuke Satan, plead the blood of Christ, and claim the victory![33]

There is perhaps nothing that could help less. Where in Scriptures are there instructions for a Christian to rebuke

Satan? How should one go about it? How does a believer plead the blood of Christ? This is no doubt a reference to Revelation 12:11,[34] which is hardly applicable to a believer indwelt by the Spirit living in the Dispensation of Grace. Any form of incantation avails nothing. It is dangerous because it takes the Christian's mind off the nature and purpose of the Scriptural defenses.

THE PURPOSE OF THE DEFENSES

The purpose for putting on the whole armor of God is stated four times in the context of Ephesians 6:10-17. The unequivocal purpose is that a believer may *stand*—that is, not be moved spiritually from the place of dependence on God—when confronted by Satanic temptations.

Note the purpose stated again and again. Verse 11 states:

…that ye may be able to stand against the wiles of the devil.

The purpose is seen in the words πρὸς τὸ δύνασθαι ὑμᾶς στῆναι. The infinitive is used most commonly to show purpose.[35]

Verse 13 states:

… that ye may be able to withstand in the evil day…

ἵνα δυνηθῆτε ἀντιστῆναι ἐν τῇ ἡμέρᾳ τῇ πονηρᾷ. The ἵνα clause shows again the clear purpose of taking up the whole armor of God.[36] Again in verse 13, the infinitive στῆτε shows purpose:

...and having done all, to stand.

In verse 14, the command to stand is given:

Stand therefore, having your loins girt about with truth, and having on the breastplate of righteousness.

The imperative στῆναι underscores the fact that if one is to be obedient to the Lord, he must stand in the day of temptation.

It is apparent that it is incumbent on every believer to stand or resist the devil's wiles (James 4:7).[37] The word for stand comes from ἵστημι, which is the most common word in the Scriptures for the physical act of standing (see Matthew 27:11; Mark 10:49; Luke 7:38; John 11:56; Acts 1:11). The word is used in a metaphorical sense of a disposition of mind that remains and will not be moved. It is used this way approximately 18 times in the Epistles.[38]

At this point, the question is: What is a Christian standing against?

THE NATURE OF THE DEFENSES

The believer is commanded to stand—but how? And how does the armor cause one to stand? The nature of the defenses is impossible to understand unless there is a clear understanding of the nature of the temptations. The nature of the temptations, as has been previously stated, refers to mental attitudes or thoughts placed in the mind of the Christian by Satan. The purpose is to entice the child of God to act independently of God and thus interrupt the believer's walking by the Holy Spirit (Galatians 5:16).

Since the armor of God is designed to render these temptations ineffective, they must be themselves weapons that fortify the tempted with proper and adequate mental attitudes to meet the test of the evil day.

The very nature of the defenses indicates a Christian is not constantly a soldier. These defenses are definite, conscious, concerted, spiritual (mental or belonging to the mind, Ephesians 4:23)[39] thought processes. They need not and cannot be around-the-clock dispositions. They are used only when one is tempted.

THE ARMOR OF GOD

Ephesians 6:14-17 states:

> *Stand therefore, having your loins girt about with truth, and having on the breastplate of righteousness;*[15] *And your feet shod with the preparation of the gospel of peace;*[16] *Above all, taking the shield of faith, wherewith ye shall be able to quench all the fiery darts of the wicked.*[17] *And take the*

helmet of salvation. and the sword of the Spirit, which is the word of God:...

William Gurnell, in 1845, published a volume on verses 10-20, and gave it the title, *The Christian in Complete Armour*. The pages are 6 inches long, and nearly 4 inches wide, and there are 827 of them. There are, on an average, 62 lines to a page, and 15 words to a line, which means 930 words to a page; that is, about 770,000 words in all. There were no penny pamphlets on big subjects in those days![40]

The reader is asked to consider the penny pamphlet that unfolds ahead!

Paul says the Christian wrestles with his spiritual foes, but in this wrestling match the believer is obliged to wear armor. The image of a wrestling match was perhaps in Paul's mind because the activity is highly personal. Wrestling produces close contact. There are many athletic contests in which the outcome does not depend completely on one individual. In wrestling this is not so. Satanic temptations, while specific in number, are adapted to every person's peculiar idiosyncrasies.

The devil has had a few thousand years to observe mankind in general. Through his demons he could no doubt produce a file on every Christian. He knows from observation what makes them happy and sad. Therefore, he can plan his methods accordingly. Richard Baxter makes an interesting comment concerning this when he says:

He [the devil] will cheat you of your faith or innocence before you are aware of it. He will make you believe it is multiplied or increased even after it is lost. You shall see neither hood nor line, much less the subtle angler himself, while he is offering you his bait. And his bait shall be so fitted to your temper and disposition that he will be sure to find advantages within you and thus make your own principles and inclinations betray you. And whenever he prevails against you, he will make you the instrument of your own ruin.[41]

Therefore, the Christian must resist, not in his own strength, but using the armor supplied by God.

Paul pictures a soldier in full armor and ready for warfare. The emphasis is upon the whole armor, even though the pieces are discussed separately. The particular location or function of the physical armor is not important to the spiritual battle in view. Each piece of armor is the same in that they are all spiritual (rational or mental) attitudes that can counter Satan's attacks. Some writers, for example, refer to the helmet of salvation as guarding the thoughts and the breastplate of righteousness as guarding the heart. It is an interesting approach, but it begins to lose appeal when it is recalled that all the armor deals with thoughts or attitudes. It seems best to see the distinctions not in the physical location of the armor, but in the quality describing each part. The following words should be stressed:

1. Truth
2. Righteousness
3. Preparation of the Gospel
4. Faith
5. Salvation
6. The Word of God

The apostle begins the armor in logical order, as he selects first the girdle of truth.

The girdle of truth

Stand therefore, having your loins girt about with truth... (Ephesians 6:14).

As previously mentioned, the purpose is to stand. Before a Christian stands, he must have previously (περιζωσάμενοι) girt himself about with truth. Truth is an actual, factual representation of the situation under consideration. It is seeing things as they actually are. When a Christian stands against Satan, it is imperative he not be deceived. This is why truth is so extremely important. When any Satanic temptation comes, a believer must first accurately analyze the situation. There is no premium for Monday morning quarterbacks in this game of life. Immediate, decisive judgment is necessary.

The mental attitude of truth will guard against all the temptations of Satan, especially those that involve truth directly, such as the temptation to lie, to tale-bear, or to be proud. Just as the Roman soldier's girdle kept the rest of his armor in place, the Christian's girdle of truth will enable him to keep the other parts of his armor properly in place. He will see each temptation as it really is.

How is an attitude of truth developed? Absolute truth is found in Jesus Christ (John 14:6)[42] and in the inerrant Word that reveals Him (John 17:17).[43] A child of God must develop and correct his view of truth from the Scriptures.

All scripture is given by inspiration of God, and is profitable for doctrine, for reproof, for correction, for instruction in righteousness:[17] *That the man of God may be perfect, thoroughly furnished unto all good works. (2 Timothy 3:16-17).*

By developing his spiritual faculties in this way, the Christian will be able to unmask Satan's deceptions. He will learn to react to situations spiritually or rationally rather than emotionally. After seeing things accurately, the Christian is ready to put on the breastplate of righteousness.

The breastplate of righteousness

Stand therefore, having on the breastplate of righteousness… (Ephesians 6:14).

The Christian is to put on the breastplate of righteousness before he stands, as ἐνδυσάμενοι (the aorist participle) indicates. If a Christian attempts to stand before doing this, he is sure to fail. The righteousness in view is a mental awareness of the positional and resultant practical righteousness a Christian has because he is in Christ.[44] One is to go about his daily life with a reservoir of thoughts that can be used in times of temptation.

To put on the breastplate of righteousness, it is necessary that the Christian's mental armor be manufactured, oiled, and polished in peace time. Otherwise it will not be complete or in working condition when temptation comes. One should think about the righteousness he has in Christ and verify the truths from the Scriptures.

> *For he hath made him to be sin for us, who knew no sin; that we might be made the righteousness of God in him. (2 Corinthians 5:21).*

This disposition of mind will enable a believer to think and act right in the face of Satanic temptations, where spiritual decisions are required. This is especially applicable to stealing, for a Christian must realize this is not acting right and certainly not in keeping with his righteous standing in Christ. This type of spiritual thinking helps any who may be tempted to have an unforgiving spirit, for this attitude and action is not in keeping with his position either.

The believer should realize that his right conduct is because of the righteousness God has given him and the empowerment of the Holy Spirit. The Christian who is acting right will be ready to bring the good news to others.

The Gospel shoes

One of the reasons God left his children on earth after salvation is so they may be witnesses and bring the Gospel to others (Acts 1:8; Titus 2:12; 1 Peter 3:15). Therefore, it is stated:

And your feet shod with the preparation of the gospel of peace... (Ephesians 6:15).

The feet must be in a state of readiness (ὑποσάμενοι) before a stand can be taken against the devil. Many opportunities for bringing the Gospel to others are lost after Satan brings a temptation to be cowardly in spiritual things.

Be not thou therefore ashamed of the testimony of our Lord, nor of me his prisoner: but be thou partaker of the afflictions of the gospel according to the power of God... (2 Timothy 1:8).

Without adequate preparation, one will not be ready (ἑτοιμασία) to give the Gospel. Robertson comments, "Readiness of mind that comes from the gospel whose message is peace."[45]

Satanic pressures can easily divert a saint from witnessing as directed by the Holy Spirit if he is not determined in his mind to follow through. The mental effort required to prepare will guard against laziness in spiritual things as well.

The shield of faith

It seems rather strange to find faith listed among the armor. Faith is basic to all the pieces of armor. The fact a person is walking by means of the Spirit indicates he has faith.

> *But the fruit of the Spirit is love, joy, peace, longsuffering, gentleness, goodness, faith... (Galatians 5:22).*

Nonetheless faith is required:

> *Above all, taking the shield of faith, wherewith ye shall be able to quench all the fiery darts of the wicked. (Ephesians 6:16).*

Emphasis on faith in this context is seen in the words *above all* (ἐν πᾶσιν), literally *in all*. This means that in the face of all temptations, the shield of faith should be up to ensure the effectiveness of the other pieces of armor. If faith is not strong during temptation, one of Satan's fiery darts may penetrate and ruin the otherwise adequate defense. Scripture defines faith as the reality of things hoped for and the proof of things not seen.

> *Now faith is the substance of things hoped for, the evidence of things not seen. (Hebrews 11:1).*

During temptation, a believer has doubt as to the reality of ultimate victory. This doubt is a fiery dart that can mentally set the soul aflame, disrupting conscious application of the other pieces of armor. The purpose of the shield is to quench, or render ineffective, the darts of the devil.

Faith, like the other parts of the spiritual armor, has its basis in the Word of God (Romans 10:17);[46] therefore, a Christian must realize that the effectiveness of his spiritual armor is directly proportional to his understanding and appropriate application of the Word to his life. The Scriptures reveal examples of how God has taken care of His believing people; these are rich sources the Christian can use to strengthen his faith.

The helmet of salvation

It is difficult to determine which piece of armor is most valuable, for they each have their own place of prominence. The helmet of salvation, however, seems to set the pattern for the rest of the defenses against the devil.

And take the helmet of salvation… (Ephesians 6:17).

The taking of the helmet of salvation is not related grammatically in the same way as the other armor. The previously mentioned armor required action prior to the verb *stand* in verse 14. This does not mean that a believer can expect to stand effectively without the helmet of salvation; it only means the helmet is related in a slightly different way, perhaps to show the importance of this particular defense.

The helmet of salvation apparently includes the salient features of the content of salvation a believer receives in this dispensation. First Thessalonians 5:8 uses the terms *helmet, the hope of salvation* in reference to the church being saved from wrath. The *helmet* in 1 Thessalonians 5:8 is anarthrous and means one of perhaps several things. (*"But let us, who are of the day, be sober, putting on the breastplate of faith and love; and for an helmet, the hope of salvation."*) The hope of the Rapture is but one thing in the Christian's content of salvation.

The Scripture declares in Ephesians 1:3 that we have been blessed with all spiritual blessings. The verb is in the past tense, and we got all of them. In this sense, God does not bless us now because we got all the blessings at the moment we became a believer in Christ. It is our responsibility to study so we are knowledgeable of all the blessings we have received.

The word *blessings* is special, meaning that God has said *good words* about us. Our English word *eulogy*—a speech about a person at his funeral—comes from this Greek word. In other words, we say good words about the deceased. The helmet of salvation then is knowing and thinking about all the things God has said about us as believers in Him. Several of these blessings are:

1. We are in the eternal plan of God.
   And we know that all things work together for good to them that love God, to them who are the called according

to his purpose.[29] For whom he did foreknow, he also did predestinate to be conformed to the image of his Son, that he might be the firstborn among many brethren.[30] Moreover whom he did predestinate, them he also called: and whom he called, them he also justified: and whom he justified, them he also glorified. (Romans 8:28-30).

2. We have been redeemed.
   Forasmuch as ye know that ye were not redeemed with corruptible things, as silver and gold, from your vain conversation received by tradition from your fathers... (1 Peter 1:18).

3. We have been reconciled.
   And you, that were sometime alienated and enemies in your mind by wicked works, yet now hath he reconciled. (Colossians 1:21).

4. We are related to God through propitiation.
   And he is the propitiation for our sins: and not for ours only, but also for the sins of the whole world. (1 John 2:2).

5. We have been forgiven all trespasses.
   And you, being dead in your sins and the uncircumcision of your flesh, hath he quickened together with him, having forgiven you all trespasses... (Colossians 2:13).

6. We have been co-joined to Christ for judgment of the old man.
   Therefore we are buried with him by baptism into death: that like as Christ was raised up from the dead by the glory of the Father, even so we also should walk in newness of life. (Romans 6:4).

7. We have been freed from the Law.
   But now we are delivered from the law, that being dead wherein we were held; that we should serve in newness of spirit, and not in the oldness of the letter. (Romans 7:6).

8. We have been made children of God.
   Behold, what manner of love the Father hath bestowed upon us, that we should be called the sons (in Greek, children) of God: therefore the world knoweth us not, because it knew him not. (1 John 3:1).

9. We have been adopted.
   For ye have not received the spirit of bondage again to fear; but ye have received the Spirit of adoption, whereby we cry, Abba, Father. (Romans 8:15).

10. We have been made righteous.
    For as by one man's disobedience many were made sinners, so by the obedience of one shall many be made righteous. (Romans 5:19).

11. We have been positionally sanctified.
    And such were some of you: but ye are washed, but ye are sanctified, but ye are justified in the name of the Lord Jesus, and by the Spirit of our God. (1 Corinthians 6:11).

12. We have been perfected forever.
    For by one offering he hath perfected forever them that are sanctified. (Hebrews 10:14).

13. We have been made accepted in the beloved.
    To the praise of the glory of his grace, wherein he hath made us accepted in the beloved. (Ephesians 1:6).

14. We have been made to meet.
    Giving thanks unto the Father, which hath made us meet to be partakers of the inheritance of the saints in light… (Colossians 1:12).

15. We have been justified.
    Being justified freely by his grace through the redemption that is in Christ Jesus… (Romans 3:24).

16. We have been made nigh.
    But now in Christ Jesus ye who sometimes were far off are made nigh by the blood of Christ. (Ephesians 2:13).

17. We have been delivered from the power of darkness.
    Who hath delivered us from the power of darkness, and hath translated us into the kingdom of his dear Son… (Colossians 1:13).

18. We have been translated into the Son's kingdom.
    Who hath delivered us from the power of darkness, and hath translated us into the kingdom of his dear Son… (Colossians 1:13).

19. We have been placed on the rock.
    Wherefore also it is contained in the scripture, Behold, I lay in Sion a chief corner stone, elect, precious: and he that believeth on him shall not be confounded. (1 Peter 2:8).

20. We have been given the glory of God.
    And the glory which thou gavest me I have given them; that they may be one, even as we are one… (John 17:22).

21. We have been circumcised in Christ.
    In whom also ye are circumcised with the circumcision made without hands, in putting off the body of the sins of the flesh by the circumcision of Christ… (Colossians 2:11).

22. We are partakers of holy and royal priesthood.
    But ye are a chosen generation, a royal priesthood, an holy nation, a peculiar people; that ye should shew forth the

praises of him who hath called you out of darkness into his marvelous light… (1 Peter 2:9).

23. We are a chosen generation, a holy nation, a particular people.
But ye are a chosen generation, a royal priesthood, an holy nation, a peculiar people; that ye should shew forth the praises of him who hath called you out of darkness into his marvelous light… (1 Peter 2:9).

24. We are heavenly citizens.
For our conversation is in heaven; from whence also we look for the Savior, the Lord Jesus Christ… (Philippians 3:20).

25. We are of the family and household of God.
Now therefore ye are no more strangers and foreigners, but fellow citizens with the saints, and of the household of God… (Ephesians 2:19).

26. We are in the fellowship of the saints.
Now therefore ye are no more strangers and foreigners, but fellow citizens with the saints, and of the household of God… (Ephesians 2:19).

27. We are in a heavenly association.
So we, being many, are one body in Christ, and every one members one of another. (Romans 12:5).

28. We have access to God.

   By whom also we have access by faith into this grace wherein we stand, and rejoice in hope of the glory of God. (Romans 5:2).

29. We are within the care of God.

   But not as the offence, so also is the free gift. For if through the offence of one many be dead, much more the grace of God, and the gift by grace, which is by one man, Jesus Christ, hath abounded unto many. (Romans 5:15).

30. We are His inheritance.

   The eyes of your understanding being enlightened; that ye may know what is the hope of his calling, and what the riches of the glory of his inheritance in the saints... (Ephesians 1:18).

31. We are in the inheritance of the saints.

   In whom also we have obtained an inheritance, being predestinated according to the purpose of him who worketh all things after the counsel of his own will... (Ephesians 1:11).

32. We are in the light of the Lord.

   Ye are all the children of light, and the children of the day: we are not of the night, nor of darkness. (1 Thessalonians 5:5).

33. We are vitally united with the Godhead.
    One God and Father of all, who is above all, and through all, and in you all. (Ephesians 4:6).

    That good thing which was committed unto thee keep by the Holy Ghost which dwelleth in us. (2 Timothy 1:14).

    To whom God would make known what is the riches of the glory of this mystery among the Gentiles; which is Christ in you, the hope of glory… (Colossians 1:27).

34. We are given the earnestness of the Spirit.
    Who hath also sealed us, and given the earnest of the Spirit in our hearts. (2 Corinthians 1:22).

35. We are glorified.
    Moreover whom he did predestinate, them he also called: and whom he called, them he also justified: and whom he justified, them he also glorified. (Romans 8:30).

36. We are complete in Him.
    And ye are complete in him, which is the head of all principality and power… (Colossians 2:10).

37. We possess every spiritual blessing.
    Blessed be the God and Father of our Lord Jesus Christ, who hath blessed us with all spiritual blessings in heavenly places in Christ… (Ephesians 1:3).

38. We are placed as a mature son.
For ye are all the children of God by faith in Christ Jesus.[27] For as many of you as have been baptized into Christ have put on Christ.[28] There is neither Jew nor Greek, there is neither bond nor free, there is neither male nor female: for ye are all one in Christ Jesus. (Galatians 3:26-28).

Now I say, That the heir, as long as he is a child, differeth nothing from a servant, though he be lord of all;[2] But is under tutors and governors until the time appointed of the father.[3] Even so we, when we were children, were in bondage under the elements of the world:[4] But when the fulness of the time was come, God sent forth his Son, made of a woman, made under the law,[5] To redeem them that were under the law, that we might receive the adoption of sons.[6] And because ye are sons, God hath sent forth the Spirit of his Son into your hearts, crying, Abba, Father.[7] Wherefore thou art no more a servant, but a son; and if a son, then an heir of God through Christ. (Galatians 4:1-7).

39. We are provided with a spiritual gift.
But now hath God set the members every one of them in the body, as it hath pleased him. (1 Corinthians 12:18).

And God hath set some in the church, first apostles, secondarily prophets, thirdly teachers, after that miracles, then gifts of healings, helps, governments, diversities of tongues. (1 Corinthians 12:28).

For as we have many members in one body, and all members have not the same office:⁵ So we, being many, are one body in Christ, and every one members one of another.⁶ Having then gifts differing according to the grace that is given to us, whether prophecy, let us prophesy according to the proportion of faith;⁷ Or ministry, let us wait on our ministering: or he that teacheth, on teaching;⁸ Or he that exhorteth, on exhortation: he that giveth, let him do it with simplicity; he that ruleth, with diligence; he that sheweth mercy, with cheerfulness. (Romans 12:4-8).

40. We are made part of the building of God.
In whom all the building fitly framed together groweth unto an holy temple in the Lord:²² In whom ye also are builded together for an habitation of God through the Spirit. (Ephesians 2:21-22).

In order to fortify one's mind against the temptation to be proud or become discouraged, a child of God must think upon the things God has given him as part of his salvation.

For example, Romans 8:29 indicates a believer in Christ has a new purpose as part of his salvation. That purpose is to be conformed to the image of the Son of God. The *all things* of Romans 8:28 are said to be good because they conform the believer to the image of Christ in this life. Discouragement is usually caused by things that come into a Christian's life to which he cannot adjust or for which he is not thankful. Realizing that God was interested enough in him to bring these particular things into his life to make him more like Christ demonstrates proper use of the helmet of salvation. This defense also guards against age conforming, because proper emphasis on the content of salvation in this dispensation will keep a believer satisfied with what God wants him to be. He will do without an age-conforming, autonomous career.

The sword of the Spirit

And take the helmet of salvation, and the sword of the Spirit, which is the word of God... (Ephesians 6:17).

This piece of equipment can be used for defense as well as offense. The sword of the Spirit is actually the sayings of God. The word translated *word* is ῥῆμα, which refers to specific statements in the Scriptures. This word differs from the word λόγος, which carries with it the idea of thought and looks at the idea or argument of a passage of Scripture. Christ used the sayings of God in His temptations. When Satan tempted Him, He said:

...It is written, Man shall not live by bread alone, but by every word that proceedeth out of the mouth of God. (Matthew 4:4).

He again used Scripture in verses seven and ten. He was not quoting Scripture to scare off Satan but rather reinforce His own human nature in this time of testing.

Christians should use the Scriptures in a similar way when undergoing temptation. It is a good way to use memorized Scriptures. The sword of the Spirit may be used against any of the wiles of the devil. There are passages in the Word of God to meet every possible temptation, but the child of God must have a working knowledge of them before temptation comes.

Through spiritual resisting, Satan will flee (James 4:7).[47] Then a Christian should pray and supplicate for others.

THE PLACE OF PRAYER AND SUPPLICATION

Ephesians 6:18 states:

Praying always with all prayer and supplication in the Spirit, and watching thereunto with all perseverance and supplication for all saints.

The purpose of prayer in regard to Satanic temptation is not because of the little poem, "Satan trembles when he sees, the weakest saint upon his knees." The purpose of prayer and supplication is not to be delivered from temptation. The spiritual armor is sufficient for this. After Satan flees, prayer should be an act of worship and praise for the victory over temptation. The supplication is for all the saints who may be experiencing temptation themselves. Paul requested the Ephesian Christians supplicate for him in regard to his ministry for the Lord. No doubt Satan was hindering in some aspect of Paul's work and ministry for the Lord. Paul was put in jail for revealing the mystery of the Gospel. Actually, the word *Gospel* in this context means the *good news* that God had set aside Israel for a time and was developing the Body of Christ, the Church.

And for me, that utterance may be given unto me, that I may open my mouth boldly, to make known the mystery of the gospel,[20] For which I am an ambassador in bonds: that therein I may speak boldly, as I ought to speak. (Ephesians 6:19-20).

Crying out, Men of Israel, help: This is the man, that teacheth all men every where against the people, and the law, and this place: and further brought Greeks also into the temple, and hath polluted this holy place. (Acts 21:28).

THE SOBER-MINDED CHRISTIAN

Satanic temptations are designed to remove the Spirit-walking Christian from a place of dependence to a place of independence from God. Satan will endeavor to tempt when least expected. The Christian must be alert in order to understand himself and the specific temptation brought before him.

The importance of sober-mindedness cannot be overemphasized. One of the leading causes of worry is lack of sober-mindedness.

Be sober, be vigilant; because your adversary the devil, as a roaring lion, walketh about, seeking whom he may devour... (1 Peter 5:7).

Sober-mindedness is not synonymous with having a long face or being sad. Sober-mindedness, or self-control, is necessary to guard against being cowardly in spiritual matters.

For God hath not given us the spirit of fear; but of power, and of love, and of a sound mind.[8] Be not thou therefore ashamed of the testimony of our Lord, nor of me his prisoner: but be thou partaker of the afflictions of the gospel according to the power of God... (2 Timothy 1:7-8).

The ability to serve the Lord in a Spirit-directed way, in contrast to age-conforming service, is based upon soberness of mind (Romans 12: 3-8).

The act of teaching others to be sober-minded is classified by Paul as *sound doctrine* (Titus 2:1, 4, 6). The grace of God teaches Christians to live soberly in this evil age.

Teaching us that, denying ungodliness and worldly lusts, we should live soberly, righteously, and godly, in this present world... (Titus 2:12).

The believer cannot produce the armor by mere positive thinking, but he can apply the armor by thinking about those things God has provided in His Word. Victory is not difficult if the right armor is properly used by the sober-minded believer.

Endnotes

1. J. Dwight Pentecost, *Your Adversary the Devil* (Grand Rapids: Zondervan Publishing House, 1969), Introduction.
2. Lewis Sperry Chafer, *Satan* (Grand Rapids: Dunham Publishing Co., 1919), p. 71.
3. Henry M. Morris, *Studies in the Bible and Science* (Grand Rapids: Baker Book House, 1966), p. 98.
4. The writer assumes Satan is seen in the Ezek. 28:11-19 and Isa. 14:12-17 accounts. For a somewhat different point of view the reader should consider "In Eden, The Garden of God: A Study of Ezekiel 28: 13" by William Dennis Barrick (an unpublished Master of Divinity critical monograph, San Francisco Baptist Theological Seminary, 1971).
5. Frank S. Mead (ed.), *Encyclopedia of Religious Quotations* (London: Peter Davies, 1965), p. 113.
6. S.I. McMillen, *None of These Diseases* (Westwood, New Jersey: Fleming H. Revell Co., 1963), p. 41.
7. John Edmund Haggai, *How to Win Over Worry* (Grand Rapids, Michigan: Zondervan Books, 1959). pp. 9-27.
8. *This I say then, Walk in the Spirit, and ye shall not fulfil the lust of the flesh. (Galatians 5:16).*
9. *That we henceforth be no more children, tossed to and fro, and carried about with every wind of doctrine, by the sleight of men, and cunning craftiness, whereby they lie in wait to deceive. (Ephesians 4:14).*
10. Archibald Thomas Robertson, *Word Pictures in the New Testament,* IV (Nashville: Broadman Press, 1931), 538.
11. W. E. Vine, *An Expository Dictionary of New Testament Words,* IV (Old Tappan, New Jersey: Fleming H. Revell Co., 1940), 216.

12 *Lest Satan should get an advantage of us: for we are not ignorant of his devices. (2 Corinthians 2:11).*
13 Vine, *An Expository*, I, 168.
14 G. Abbott-Smith, *A Manual Greek Lexicon of the New Testament* (Edinburgh: T. & T. Clark, 1921), p. 32.
15 Kenneth S. Wuest, *First Peter in the Greek New Testament for the English Reader* (Grand Rapids: Wm. B. Eerdmans Publishing Co., 1942), p. 129.
16 Donald Grey Barnhouse, *The Invisible War* (Grand Rapids: Zondervan Publishing House, 1965), p. 176.
17 Robertson, *Word Pictures*, IV, 573.
18 *In whom the god of this world hath blinded the minds of them which believe not, lest the light of the glorious gospel of Christ, who is the image of God, should shine unto them. (2 Corinthians 4:4).*
19 *Now to him that worketh is the reward not reckoned of grace, but of debt. (Romans 4:4).*
20 *I thank God through Jesus Christ our Lord. So then with the mind I myself serve the law of God; but with the flesh the law of sin. (Romans 7:25).*
21 *For I say, through the grace given unto me, to every man that is among you, not to think of himself more highly than he ought to think; but to think soberly, according as God hath dealt to every man the measure of faith.[4] For as we have many members in one body, and all members have not the same office:[5] So we, being many, are one body in Christ, and every one members one of another.[6] Having then gifts differing according to the grace that is given to us, whether prophecy, let us prophesy according to the proportion of faith... (Romans 12:3-6).*
22 Haggai, *Win Over Worry*, p. 14.

23 *Peter said unto him, Lord, why cannot I follow thee now? I will lay down my life for thy sake. (John 13:37).*
24 James Hope Moulton and George Milligan, *The Vocabulary of the Greek Testament* (Grand Rapids: Wm. B. Eerdmans Publishing Co., 1963), p. 221.
25 Homer A. Kent, Jr., *The Pastoral Epistles* (Chicago: Moody Press, 1958), p. 257.
26 Marvin R. Vincent, *World Studies in the New Testament*, I (Grand Rapids: Wm. B. Eerdmans Publishing Co., 1946), 467.
27 Robertson, *Word*, IV, 586.
28 *But the younger widows refuse: for when they have begun to wax wanton against Christ, they will marry;[12] Having damnation, because they have cast off their first faith.[13] And withal they learn to be idle, wandering about from house to house; and not only idle, but tattlers also and busybodies, speaking things which they ought not.[14] I will therefore that the younger women marry, bear children, guide the house, give none occasion to the adversary to speak reproachfully.[15] For some are already turned aside after Satan. (1 Timothy 5:11-15).*
29 Robertson, Word, IV, 586.
30 Kenneth S. Wuest, *The Pastoral Epistles in the Greek New Testament* (Grand Rapids: Wm. B. Eerdmans Publishing Co., 1964), p. 84.
31 *For we hear that there are some which walk among you disorderly, working not at all, but are busybodies. (2 Thessalonians 3:11).*
32 H.L. Wilmington. "If I Were the Devil," *Baptist Bulletin*, (December 1971), p. 14.
33 Ibid., pg. 13.

34 *And they overcame him by the blood of the Lamb, and by the word of their testimony; and they loved not their lives unto the death. (Revelation 12:11).*
35 H. E. Dana and Julius R. Mantey, *A Manual Grammar of the Greek New Testament* (New York: The Macmillan Co., 1927), p. 214.
36 Eugene Van Ness Goetchius, *The Language of the New Testament* (New York: Charles Scribner's Sons, 1965), p. 271.
37 *Submit yourselves therefore to God. Resist the devil, and he will flee from you. (James 4:7).*
38 Note Romans 3:31, 5:2, 10:3, 11:20, 14:4; 1 Corinthians 7:37, 10:12, 15:1; 2 Corinthians 1:24, 13:1; Ephesians 6:11, 13, 14; Colossians 4:12; 2 Timothy 2:19; 1 Peter 5:12.
39 *And be renewed in the spirit of your mind... (Ephesians 4:23).*
40 W. Graham Scroggie, *The Unfolding Drama of Redemption*, (Old Tappan, New Jersey: Fleming H. Revell Co., 1970), p. 198.
41 Richard Baxter, *The Reformed Pastor* (Grand Rapids: Sovereign Grace Publishers, 1971), p. 7.
42 *Jesus saith unto him, I am the way, the truth, and the life: no man cometh unto the Father, but by me. (John 14:6).*
43 *Sanctify them through thy truth: thy word is truth. (John 17:17).*
44 Charles Caldwell Ryrie, *Balancing the Christian Life* (Chicago: Moody Press, 1969), p. 133.
45 Robertson, *Word*, IV, 551.
46 *So then faith cometh by hearing, and hearing by the word of God. (Romans 10:17).*
47 *Submit yourselves therefore to God. Resist the devil, and he will flee from you. (James 4:7).*

CHAPTER 3

THE CHRISTIAN'S DEFENSE AGAINST THE WORLD

The ship's place is in the sea, but God pity the ship when the sea gets into it. The Christian's place is in the world, but God pity the Christian if the world gets the best of him.

Anonymous

The Meaning of the Word *World*

Perhaps the greatest problem with enemy number three is the difficulty one has in properly identifying it. The word *world* is used four different ways in the New Testament.

THE CREATED UNIVERSE

The word κόσμος refers to an ordered system and depends upon the context to determine the exact meaning or way it is used. The term κόσμος has a long, interesting history and was used often from the time of Homer up to and through the Gospels and Church Epistles period.[1]

The physical world is referred to in Ephesians 1:4:

According as he hath chosen us in him before the foundation of the world…

This was before Satan developed his cosmos system.

The Lord Jesus Christ is said to be slain before the creation of the universe.

…the Lamb slain from the foundation of the world. (Revelation 13:8).

God accounted this to have taken place long before any material universe came into existence.

THE EARTH

One key verse that uses the word *world* (κόσμος) is John 1:10:

He was in the world, and the world was made by him, and the world knew him not.

The world was made by him is a reference to the earth primarily, but perhaps could reach further to include the universe as verse three states.

Another clear statement of God creating the world is Acts 17:24:

God that made the world…

Again in Romans 5:12:

…sin entered into the world…

This phrase, of course, refers back to the garden of Eden on earth. John says that if everything Jesus did was written, there would not be room on the face of the earth to place all the rolls of writing.

And there are also many other things which Jesus did, the which, if they should be written every one, I suppose that even the world itself could not contain the books that should be written. Amen. (John 21: 25).

THE UNSAVED

The use of the word *world* to refer to those spiritually dead is common in the New Testament. The well-known John 3:16 illustrates this fact:

For God so loved the world, that he gave his only begotten Son, that whosoever believeth in him should not perish, but have everlasting life.

God did not love the Satanically devised system, but He did love the souls of men who were completely identified with it.

God reconciled the world to Himself (2 Corinthians 5:19);[2] thus, the unsaved can be saved. Perhaps the reason *cosmos* sometimes refers to unsaved individuals is because of the complete and permanent enmeshing of the lost in the world's system.

THE SYSTEM CONTROLLED BY SATAN

Most of the New Testament writers use the term κόσμος, but John stands out far above all the rest combined. In the Gospel, he uses the term 79 times, plus 23 times in his Epistles for a total of 102 occurrences.[3] Nearly 56 percent of the occurrences in the Scriptures are used by the apostle Jesus loved. The one who forcefully portrayed the deity of Christ did so with the world system as the black contrasting background. The one who spoke of fellowship saw clearly one of the great hindrances to fellowship—the world. What is the world today? It is basically governments, and in some way everyone is involved in these things in order to exist.

The World's System

1. **The Governments**
   - United Nations
   - Federal governments
   - State governments
   - County governments
   - City governments
2. **The Money System**
   - International banking system
   - The Federal Reserve
   - Local banking agencies
3. **Commerce**
   - Manufacturing
   - Transportation
   - Retail and wholesale stores
   - Hospitals and the complete medical field
4. **Professional Sports**
   - Football
   - Hockey
   - Basketball
   - Golf
   - Baseball
   - All others
5. **Entertainment**
   - Radio programs
   - Television shows

- Internet, Facebook, etc.
- Live plays
- Cell phones

6. All Tax-Supported School Systems
- Elementary schools
- High schools
- Colleges

If believers totally operate one of the above-mentioned items according the Word of God, it may not be considered part of the world system. Sometimes governments can be favorable to Christians, and sometimes they can be hostile. Governments are involved in schools and colleges. Today, schools and colleges teach things very contrary to the Bible. The brainwashing of students helps promote a dictatorship, which the devil desires.

What type of government do *the Rulers of the darkness of this World* like best? Remember, the Devil is not omniscient or all-powerful, so he has easier work to do when he has a total dictatorship. Historically, the rulers of the world have been kings and dictators.

A king is a person who can do what he wants, and the people have no say. They must obey. This is Satan's desired form of government. He can also easily work through a socialistic form of government.

Socialism can turn quickly to total dictatorship when the people cannot defend themselves. This is why socialists hate the Second Amendment in the United States. A person who is called a liberal is really a socialist. The same individuals do not want the people to own firearms.

The more a government follows the Bible, the more difficult it is for evil powers to control everything. When this country was started, not everyone was a believer, but many were and others liked the morality taught in the Scriptures. The First Amendment to the Constitution made it so the government could not support one denomination or hinder the free exercise of religion. Religion in that day meant Christianity. In 1878, the Supreme Court ruled against the practice of polygamy because they said it was "against the peace and good order."

Today, Satan's working is called the Deep State. These people have a different purpose in their job than doing what they were hired to do. Their numbers are great in size. The FBI has over 38,000 employees. At the present time, the Central Intelligence Agency has 21,000. The NSA has 30,000 to 40,000. The Secret Service has 7,000. Most of these agencies are violating the law of the land, the Constitution, by infringing on the Fourth Amendment in their unlawful spying on the people of America. From time to time, individuals in these agencies are prosecuted for crimes they have committed.

If the government becomes too destructive of individual rights, the people have a right to alter or abolish it, as Thomas Jefferson said. The people in this country are the powers that be, not the elected government or the appointed and hired individuals.

Another concept of the world system is commercial activities. These involve money transactions, from stores to entertainment like sporting events, Hollywood shows, and the little computer we carry in our pockets called a cell phone.

Jesus calls Satan *the prince of this world* (John 12: 31; 14:30; 16:11). Satan is the one who energizes the world system, for it belongs to him (Luke 4:6).

And we know that we are of God, and the whole world lieth in wickedness. (1 John 5:19).

This is shown by the fact that Christ never questioned the devil's authority over the kingdoms of the earth.

When commenting about the evilness of the cosmos, Chafer stated:

The root evil in the cosmos is that in it there is an all-comprehensive order or system which is methodized on a basis of complete independence of God.

He went on to say:

It is the consummating display of that which the creature—both angelic and human—can produce, having embarked on an autonomous career.[4]

The content of this evil age pours its supply into the works of the cosmos system.

Some of the characteristics of the world are as follows:

1. The world does not know Christ (John 1:10; 17:25).
2. The world hates Christ (John 7:7).
3. The works of the world are evil (John 7:7).
4. The world's prince is Satan (John 14:30).
5. The world hates believers (John 15:18, 17:14; 1 John 3:13).
6. The world loves its own (John 15:19).
7. The world is not prayed for by Christ (John 17:9).
8. The world by wisdom did not know God (1 Corinthians 1:21).
9. The world has its own age (Ephesians 2:2).
10. The world has its own base teaching (Colossians 2:8).
11. The world was not worthy of believers (Hebrews 11:7).
12. The world will soil a Christian (James 1:27).
13. The world is corrupt (2 Peter 1:4).
14. The world is polluted (2 Peter 2:20).
15. The world is composed of two-thirds lust and one-third pride (1 John 2:16).
16. The world will pass away (1 John 2:17).
17. The world cannot experientially know Christians (1 John 3:1).
18. The world hears its own (1 John 4:5).
19. The world lies in the lap of Satan (1 John 5:19).
20. The world has its own kingdoms (Matt. 4:8; Revelation 11:15).

One major operation of the world system is the governments of the many nations. Today, we have learned some things the Deep State is doing. The Deep State refers to hidden, often illegal, operations of government that are kept secret from the people. As communication systems expand, the many things the Deep State was doing have now been made public to some degree. We have been shocked to discover our government, in direct violation of our Bill of Rights, has been spying on us. They have been recording our phone conversations. The Deep State is afraid of the people of this country, because the people are more powerful than the state. The illegal operations of some departments have now been made known, and they would have made Al Capone green with jealousy and envy of their secret, mob-type activities. Fortunately, the U.S. Supreme Court has recently ruled against this type of spying on the people.

As Kenneth Wuest so aptly stated:

> *Kosmos* refers to an ordered system. Here it is the ordered system of which Satan is the head, his fallen angels and demons are his emissaries, and the unsaved of the human race are his subjects, together with those purposes, pursuits, pleasures, practices, and places where God is not wanted. Much in this world-system is religious, cultured, refined, and intellectual. But it is anti-God and anti-Christ.[5]

A believer is not prepared to cope with his most subtle enemy until he fully understands the gutter character of the cosmos. It is difficult, if not impossible, to separate unsaved individuals from the world's system, for the system depends on unsaved people to carry out its operations. Before the fall, Satan had never witnessed the outward activities of a sin nature. It no doubt took him by surprise. Satan's purpose, as it has been stated, was to get Adam and Eve to act independently of God—the same as he, the anointed cherub, had done. The result was a sin nature or principle that produced desires in man (please note the flesh works in Galatians 5:19-21)[6] not known before to Satan or men.

The bent to produce these works made man's corrupt nature his own god. Man may have been free to act independently of God, but he became a bond slave to his own corrupt nature. Almost immediately, as mankind was multiplying upon the face of the earth, Satan began to develop his system to direct man's sin nature into constructive channels for the advancement of the kingdom of darkness. Genesis 4:17 states:

And Cain knew his wife. and she conceived, and bare Enoch: and he builded a city, and called the name of the city, after the name of his son, Enoch.

Satan uses many things to develop his system. Some things are good in themselves. Chafer succinctly comments:

That things good in themselves are included in this great system is doubtless the occasion for many deceptions. The fundamental truth that "whatsoever is not of faith is sin" (Romans 14:23; cf. Hebrews 11:6) is not recognized or believed in the cosmos.

He continues:

The humanitarian enterprises, the culture, the laws, and religious forms of the cosmos constitute no evidence that God is recognized in His true position or honored. This is a Christ-rejecting cosmos. Its princes "crucified the Lord of glory" (1 Corinthians 2:8), and apart from the restraining power of God they would crucify Him again and destroy His witnesses. They evince no penitence for their climactic racial crime—the Savior, as such, is still disowned and rejected. Social ideals are borrowed from His teachings. His purity and grace are held forth as a pattern of life, but salvation through His blood is spurned. The independent, self-centered, self-satisfied, autonomous cosmos asks for no redemption since it recognizes no need. It is the embodiment of the philosophy of which Cain is the archetype.[7]

The Christian many times is taken out of fellowship with God by the subtle world system when his other enemies are not able to touch him.

The Christian's Relationship to the World

The Christian is certainly a unique individual upon this earth. While those unsaved about him are *in* and *of* the world, the Christian is only *in* the world. Christ asserted:

> *I have given them thy word; and the world hath hated them, because they are not of the world, even as I am not of the world… (John 17:14).*

All around the Christian lies the world's system; the Christian stands in a delicate balance—he must use the world but not abuse it.

THE USE OF THE WORLD

The right use of the world is difficult to define. Perhaps this is why in 1 Corinthians 7:31 the Scripture defines *use* by comparing it with something else:

> *And they that use this world, as not abusing it: for the fashion of this world passeth away.*

The temptations offered by the world are probably the most difficult to detect because they are so subtle. This is true because a believer must live *in* the world and *use* it, even though he is not *of* the world nor is he to use it up to the full. This borderline situation must be watched closely, and a Christian should judge himself periodically to see that this proper relationship is maintained.

The idea of using conveys exactly that:

...but use a little wine for thy stomach's sake...
(1 Timothy 5:23).

This means to partake of the wine. It should be carefully noted that most wine in Biblical times was nonalcoholic, dried grape juice to which they added water. The world system includes the culture, government, educational institutions, sports, and other forms of entertainment. It should not be understood that it is wrong to use some things of the world's system because of a supposed damaging spiritual effect. On the other hand, the concept of *using* the world must never be understood that everything in the world, at the right time and place, can be used a little. This, in the writer's opinion, has been at least one cause for spiritual decline in Bible-believing churches today. For example, some Christians have concluded that it is wrong to go to the "dirty" movies at the theater, but that it is all right to watch them at home on television. The very psychology of motion pictures requires vicarious involvement, and a Christian watching them mentally identifies with what he is observing. A little use of such things does not constitute using, but rather abusing (using to the full) the world's system.

THE ABUSE OF THE WORLD

The abuse of the world means to use it up to the full. The word is κακαχρώμενοι. The Apostle Paul uses this word in 1 Corinthians 9:18 in reference to preaching the Gospel without charge so that he would not abuse his authority in the Gospel. If he used all that was in his power, it would constitute a misuse. Moulton and Milligan illustrate the meaning of κακαχρώμενοι by saying:

> The intensive force of this compound "use up," "use to the full," which is found in 1 Cor 731, may be illustrated from P Oxy II. 28114 (A.D. 20-50) where a woman lodges a complaint against her husband..."but Sarapion, having squandered my dowry as he pleased..."[8]

Again it should not be thought that a Christian can plunge himself into the world and stop just short of doing everything the world does in order to assuage his conscience. The abuse is defined by the statements of other Scriptures. The Christian who is a friend of the world is said to be in spiritual adultery (James 4:4). Φιλία is the word for *friendship* and represents a love because of the pleasure derived from the object loved. The child of God is to receive his pleasure from God rather than the world's system. This does not mean a Christian cannot derive some pleasure from some things in the world. The context of James 4:4 indicates those who are carnal and those who have *willed* or *determined* (βουληθῇ) that the world will be their source of pleasure and friendship.

> *Ye adulterers and adulteresses, know ye not that the friendship of the world is enmity with God? whosoever therefore will be a friend of the world is the enemy of God.*

The Holy Spirit is certainly grieved at this action.

> *Do ye think that the scripture saith in vain, The spirit that dwelleth in us lusteth to envy? (James 4:5).*

The Christian who is *using the world up to the full* will exhibit the world's characteristics by showing worldly wisdom (1 Corinthians 1:20).[9] His philosophy of life will be geared toward the rudiments of the world (Colossians 2:8).[10] It is not wrong to watch a professional football game on television, but if you have to miss a church fellowship and Bible teaching time on the Lord's day to watch it, then that is abusing the system.

The temptations of the world are perhaps the easiest to overcome, but when a Christian is involved in abusing the world, he will be *spotted* (James 1:27), *corrupted* (2 Peter 1:4), *polluted* (2 Peter 2:20), and finally *have many sorrows* (1 Timothy 6:7-10). It is difficult indeed to recover from the grip of worldliness. It is far easier to overcome the temptations in the beginning.

The Temptations of the World

The temptations are perhaps best explained as static temptations. This means they do not go after and pursue the Christian; they wait for the Christian to come to them. This is different from Satanic temptations, for the devil goes about as a roaring lion seeking whom he may devour. He can place thoughts in the believer's mind, but the world must appeal to the child of God through the physical senses.

THE LUST OF THE FLESH

John says:

> *For all that is in the world, the lust of the flesh, and the lust of the eyes, and the pride of life, is not of the Father, but is of the world. (1 John 2:16).*

It is probably best to understand the phrase *the lust of the flesh* (ἡ ἐπιθυμία τῆς σαρκὸς) as a subjective genitive *(lust felt by the flesh)*.[11]

The converse is also true. The world is composed of the unsaved, who are given over to the lusts of the flesh. The world's system, under the direction and control of Satan, produces things that are a rallying point for the strong desires of the sin principle within man. After the fall, the devil recognized man's condition, so he developed a system to control him. This highly devised system, by the nature of its purpose, contained things that attract in order to control man's fleshy desires to some extent. The unsaved person and the carnal Christian fall in line with the world's system completely, and their attitude of mind is in harmony with it.

> *From whence come wars and fightings among you? come they not hence, even of your lusts that war in your members?[2] Ye lust, and have not: ye kill, and desire to have, and cannot obtain: ye fight and war, yet ye have not, because ye ask not.[3] Ye ask, and receive not, because ye ask amiss, that ye may consume it upon your lusts.[4] Ye adulterers and adulteresses, know ye not that the friendship of the world is enmity with God? whosoever therefore will be a friend of the world is the enemy of God. (James 4: 1-4).*

The Spirit-controlled Christian, on the other hand, will feel the tug of the world. Satan's supreme desire is to use the world's system to get the believer from a place of dependence on God and be independent from the Lord's restraints.

The lust of the flesh from the world's system can be illustrated by a standard article of clothing worn by most Christian girls of high school age, and many older women as well—the miniskirt, which is immodest. Styles in dress are certainly from the world's system, whether they be long or short. The Christian is obligated to use the world—you must wear clothes! But, according to the designer of the miniskirt, it was intended to bring about certain works of the flesh, namely fornication.

Police reports indicate it has been a maxi success.[12] This particular thing in the world arouses the flesh—a Christian must be sober and led of the Spirit to direct his love away from this worldliness and toward to the Father.

THE LUST OF THE EYES

The second area of worldly temptation is *the lust of the eyes*. This is the lust felt by the eyes. It should not be thought of as only using the eye gate to reach the sin principle within. That would be very redundant to say the least. John apparently uses the term *lust of the eyes* to refer to the part of one's human nature that receives pleasure from what it sees but should not be classified as a work of the flesh. An example could be recreation, sports, etc., which give pleasure to the human nature but are not themselves works of the flesh. The word *lust* is literally *strong desires,* and not necessarily bad; it must be judged by the context. There are many things in the world that provide pleasure and can be used but must not be an object of the Christian's love. When these things prevent the Christian from depending upon the Lord and being used of Him, they are out of bounds.

THE PRIDE OF LIFE

The most subtle form of the temptations of the world is *the pride of life*. This is a translation of ἡ ἀλαζονεία τοῦ βίου. Ἀλαζονεία refers to vainglory. Vincent says:

It means, originally, *empty, braggart talk or display; swagger*; and thence an insolent and vain assurance in one's own resources or in the stability of earthly things, which issues in a contempt of divine laws.[13]

It is vainglory of βίου, or those things that sustain physical life here on earth. Here again the idea of using the world comes into view. A Christian, like the unsaved, needs food, clothing, and shelter, but the things that provide for this need can be a cause for boasting. Guy King describes this as:

> …evil desires arising out of the urge for wealth, position, comfort, power. Many a man has been brought down spiritually when he has climbed up materially.[14]

Because man's human nature is fallen, he cannot control its normal desire for nourishment, clothing, or shelter by himself. Man's needs become perverted into insatiable wants. The world's system will endeavor to put false price tags on things that support physical life. Perhaps the desire for a home or car, which are legitimate needs, can consume a Christian to the point that God is not controlling his life. The system has tricked him into thinking joy and peace come from crackling logs on the fireplace rather than the Holy Spirit. The natural and good use of the world has caused him to trust in them. The Christian who is not directing his love properly can develop inordinate affections, so that he sees something precious in things that John says are in the process of passing away (1 John 2:17).[15] It is a sad condition for a believer to be drawn away in this way and lose his testimony for the Lord for:

> ...even the unsaved who live a simple life are oftentimes more content than the believer trying to keep up with the progress of a satanic society.[16]

The Defenses for Worldly Temptations

Defense against the world requires first that a believer be abiding in the Lord.

> *I write unto you, little children, because your sins are forgiven you for his name's sake.[13] I write unto you, fathers, because ye have known him that is from the beginning. I write unto you, young men, because ye have overcome the wicked one. I write unto you, little children, because ye have known the Father.[14] I have written unto you, fathers, because ye have known him that is from the beginning. I have written unto you, young men, because ye are strong, and the word of God abideth in you, and ye have overcome the wicked one. (1 John 2:12-14).*

A Christian living in sin has no protection from the world, and he is usually living for it. The fact that a Christian has positionally overcome the world should be the basis of the defense.

> *Ye are of God, little children, and have overcome them: because greater is he that is in you, than he that is in the world.[5] They are of the world: therefore speak they of the world, and the world heareth them. (1 John 5:4-5).*

Merely knowing this is not enough, for a Christian must be able to determine what the right and wrong use of the world is according to the Word of God.

BE DISCERNING

All the enemies of the Christian have the common element of disguise. They never appear as they really are to the person being tempted. When the man of God was tempted in 1 Kings 13, the appeal never gained a foothold until the temptation came masquerading in the form of the old prophet. Temptation will be as subtle as a person is spiritual. The Christian must be discerning as to what the Word of God teaches.

> *These were more noble than those in Thessalonica, in that they received the word with all readiness of mind, and searched the scriptures daily, whether those things were so. (Acts 17:11).*

If any man teach otherwise, and consent not to wholesome words, even the words of our Lord Jesus Christ, and to the doctrine which is according to godliness;[4] He is proud, knowing nothing, but doting about questions and strifes of words, whereof cometh envy, strife, railings, evil surmisings,[5] Perverse disputings of men of corrupt minds, and destitute of the truth, supposing that gain is godliness: from such withdraw thyself.[6] But godliness with contentment is great gain.[7] For we brought nothing into this world, and it is certain we can carry nothing out.[8] And having food and raiment let us be therewith content.[9] But they that will be rich fall into temptation and a snare, and into many foolish and hurtful lusts, which drown men in destruction and perdition.[10] For the love of money is the root of all evil: which while some coveted after, they have erred from the faith, and pierced themselves through with many sorrows. (1 Timothy 6:3-10).

That the man of God may be perfect, thoroughly furnished unto all good works. (2 Timothy 3:17).

It is impossible to mature and have victory over the world if one does not know how to use the world, and this factor is governed by the Scriptures.

It is also necessary to be discerning about one's self and family. Pressure from Satan's system is placed on Christian families in the form of public education. Discerning parents need to consider if utilizing the local public school system is abusing rather than using the world.

REFUSE TO LOVE THE WORLD

First John 2:15 states:

> *Love not the world, neither the things that are in the world. If any man love the world, the love of the Father is not in him.*

Love not is μη ἀγαπᾶτε, which carries the idea of *stop loving,* apparently something the Christians were already doing. This command presupposes at least three factors. First, it assumes they know what the world is and the things of which it is composed. Second, the fact that they had ἀγαπη (fruit of the Spirit) indicates they were abiding in Christ and thus could love (John 15:10-13; Romans 5:5; Galatians 5:22).

Perhaps the most important factor regarding this defense is that the Christian is responsible for directing this love properly. He is not responsible for producing the love, but for properly directing it. Paul prayed the Philippian Christians' love would abound more and more in full knowledge and perception (Philippians 1:9).[17] Love must not be ignorantly directed. If one directs his (Holy Spirit produced) love to the world, he at the same time cannot love the Father (1 John 2:15). *The love of the Father* with this idea would be understood as an objective genitive, i.e. the love is not produced by the Father but directed to Him. The Christian either loves God or the world; they are mutually exclusive. If a Christian insists upon loving the world, the Holy Spirit will be grieved to see His fruit used in this fashion.

To maintain fellowship, the Christian should love those things God loves and hate those things God hates. He should live his life in a way God would. This can only be determined by the revealed will of God in His Word and the leading of the Holy Spirit, which will be consonant with the Word. This type of spiritual exercise will produce a growing Christian and bring about the desired end God intended—the maturing Christian.

> *Till we all come in the unity of the faith, and of the knowledge of the Son of God, unto a perfect man, unto the measure of the stature of the fulness of Christ:*[14] *That we henceforth be no more children, tossed to and fro, and carried about with every wind of doctrine, by the sleight of men, and cunning craftiness, whereby they lie in wait to deceive… (Ephesians 4:13-14).*

Endnotes

1. Gerhard Kittel (ed.), *Theological Dictionary of the New Testament*, III (Grand Rapids: Wm. B. Eerdmans Publishing Co., 1965), 868.
2. *To wit, that God was in Christ, reconciling the world unto himself, not imputing their trespasses unto them; and hath committed unto us the word of reconciliation. (2 Corinthians 5:19).*
3. J. B. Smith, *Greek-English Concordance to the New Testament* (Scottdale, Pennsylvania: Herald Press, 1955), p. 206.
4. Lewis Sperry Chafer, *Systematic Theology*, II (Dallas: Dallas Seminary Press, 1947), 84.
5. Kenneth S. Wuest, *In These Last Days* (Grand Rapids: Wm. B. Eerdmans Publishing Co., 1954), p. 125.
6. *Now the works of the flesh are manifest, which are these; Adultery, fornication, uncleanness, lasciviousness,[20] Idolatry, witchcraft, hatred, variance, emulations, wrath, strife, seditions, heresies,[21] Envyings, murders, drunkenness, revellings, and such like: of the which I tell you before, as I have also told you in time past, that they which do such things shall not inherit the kingdom of God. (Galatians 5:19-21).*
7. Chafer, *Systematic*, II, 85.
8. James Hope Moulton and George Milligan, *The Vocabulary of the Greek New Testament* (Grand Rapids: Wm. B. Eerdmans Publishing Co., 1963), p. 335.
9. *Where is the wise? where is the scribe? where is the disputer of this world? hath not God made foolish the wisdom of this world? (1 Corinthians 1:20).*
10. *Beware lest any man spoil you through philosophy and vain deceit, after the tradition of men, after the rudiments of the world, and not after Christ. (Colossians 2:8).*

11 A.T. Robertson, *Word Pictures in the New Testament*, VI (Nashville: Broadman Press, 1931), 214.

12 Barton L. Collins, Chief of Detectives of the San Jose, California, Police Department, blamed miniskirt for attracting the "sex nuts to college communities." *Spartan Daily*, April 23, 1970, p. 3.

13 Marvin R. Vincent, *World Studies in the New Testament*, II (Grand Rapids: Wm. B. Eerdmans Publishing Co., 1946), p. 336.

14 Guy H. King, *The Fellowship* (London & Edinburgh: Marshall, Morgan & Scott, Ltd., 1954), p. 53.

15 *And the world passeth away, and the lust thereof: but he that doeth the will of God abideth forever. (1 John 2:17).*

16 H. L. Roush, *Henry and the Great Society* (Belpre, Ohio: By the author, 1969), p. 106.

17 *And this I pray, that your love may abound yet more and more in knowledge and in all judgment… (Philippians 1:9).*

PART TWO

SPIRITUAL MATURITY IN RELATIONSHIP TO SPIRITUAL CONFLICT

CHAPTER 4

THE BASIS OF SPIRITUAL MATURITY

Blessed is the man that endureth temptation: for when he is tried, he shall receive the crown of life, which the Lord hath promised to them that love him. (James 1:12)

Before any attempt is made to discuss the features of spiritual maturity, it is of utmost importance to consider briefly the salient elements of spiritual life. The term *spiritual life* as used in this book refers to the life that is properly related to the Holy Spirit, so spiritual maturity may result. Spiritual maturity should be the ultimate norm for every Christian. It is not just for spiritual leaders (so-called), but for all Christians without regard to office or function.

Many Bible-believing churches have structures that make the practical emphasis of true spiritual growth go into eclipse.[1] This is caused by practical denial of the priesthood of the believer by focusing on one "protestant priest" who runs the show. God desires that all Christians worship in spirit and in truth and offer spiritual sacrifices well-pleasing to the Lord Jesus Christ. There is a place of true spiritual service for every believer.

The Spirit-Controlled Christian

Much has been written concerning spiritual life—or it could be said *the contemporary pious life.* Though much has been said about spiritual life which would lead one to believe the profundity of the subject is something to behold, the contrary is the case.

The key passage in the New Testament enjoining Spirit-filling or Spirit-control is Ephesians 5:18:

> *And be not drunk with wine, wherein is excess; but be filled with the Spirit.*

The normal sense for understanding this verse is to see the comparison between the word *drunk* and the word *filled.* It is an all too frequent occurrence to observe someone walking down the street who is intoxicated with alcohol. The alcohol, in a real sense, *controls* this person. His walk is unsteady, for he staggers; his talk is loose, for his tongue moves uncoordinatedly; his judgment is impaired as his brain becomes further affected. Thus, everything about a drunk is affected. In a similar sense, if a Christian is filled with the Spirit, his whole life—walk, talk, and judgment—is affected. He is controlled by the Spirit. The Son of God is being manifested in his life—for the Spirit of God will produce love, joy, peace, longsuffering, gentleness, goodness, faith, meekness, and temperance.

> *But the fruit of the Spirit is love, joy, peace, longsuffering, gentleness, goodness, faith,[23] Meekness, temperance: against such there is no law. (Galatians 5:22-23).*

While a Christian is being controlled by the Spirit, he will be involved simultaneously in meaningful inward spiritual exercises, such as singing, speaking psalms, and submitting as the present participle in Ephesians 5:18, 19 indicates. The impact of the word *filled* (πληροῦσθε) is significant here, as Wuest points out:

> There are four grammatical rules in the Greek language which lead us to four truths relative to this great subject. The words in Ephesians 5:18 are, "Be filled with the Spirit." First, the verb is in the imperative mood. That is, it is imperative that we be filled with the Spirit, first, because God commands it, second, because the fullness of the spirit is the divine enablement in the life of a Christian which results in a Christ-like life. Failure to be filled with the Spirit is sin and results in failure to live a life honoring to God.

Second, the tense of the verb is present, and this tense in the imperative mode always represents action going on. We learn from this that the mechanics of a Spirit-filled life do not provide for a spasmodic filling, that is, the Christian is not filled only when doing service such as preaching or teaching. But the Christian living a normal life of moment by moment to God, experiences a moment by moment fullness of the Spirit. No Christian can do with less and at the same time live a victorious life.

Third, the verb is in the plural number, which teaches us that this command is addressed, not only to the preacher and the deacon, and the teacher in the Sunday School, but to every Christian, to the business man, the laborer, the housewife. It is the responsibility of every Christian to be always filled with the Holy Spirit.

Fourth, the verb is in the passive voice. This grammatical classification represents the subject of the verb as inactive but being acted upon. This teaches us that the filling with the Spirit is not a work of man but of God.[2]

The Spirit-controlled life is the expected thing; it is the only life acceptable to God because it is by an attitude of faith (Hebrews 11:6).[3] Every Christian, young or old, can be filled with the Spirit. Sin is the only thing that will keep a

Christian from being Spirit-filled, and thus wreck the path leading to maturity.

SIN

Sin is a very misunderstood term today. The worldly person looks at sin and calls it a mistake, or perhaps a sickness, or worse yet "only being human." Even in Bible-believing circles, the word is misused. In the minds of many, the idea of sin is anything displeasing to God. The New Testament is clear in defining sin. The Scripture presents sin as one specific entity. First John 3:4, literally translated, says:

Everyone doing the sin also does the lawlessness and the sin is the lawlessness.

The idea is that sin means throwing off the restraints (or law) God has placed upon a person. Sin also involves knowledge and a willful determination to carry out the action against a stated restriction given by God (James 4:17; Romans 5:13, 7:7). When a Christian sins, he is immediately out of fellowship with the Lord and is in need of forgiveness. Sin is the only thing that breaks fellowship with God.

If we say that we have fellowship with him, and walk in darkness, we lie, and do not the truth:[7] But if we walk in the light, as he is in the light, we have fellowship one with another, and the blood of Jesus Christ his Son cleanseth us from all sin.[8] If we say that we have no sin, we deceive ourselves, and the truth is not in us.[9] If we confess our sins, he is faithful and just to forgive us our sins, and to cleanse us from all unrighteousness. (1 John 1:6-9).

The road to spiritual maturity requires knowledge of how to have victory over sin. There is little possibility of true growth if a Christian's spiritual life is characterized by a repeating cycle of temporary victory and inevitable defeat, like the rises and dips of a roller coaster. There must be stability; confession and forgiveness are necessary to have this virtue.

CONFESSION AND FORGIVENESS

If we confess our sins, he is faithful and just to forgive us our sins, and to cleanse us from all unrighteousness. (1 John 1:9).

The Christian is not called to ask for forgiveness; he is merely to confess (ὁμολογῶμεν). Confession means to name your sins to God and to have the same attitude about them as God has. Wuest says:

The saint is to confess. The word "confess" is *homologeō*, from *homos*, "the same" and *legō*, "to say" thus, "to say the same thing as another," or "to agree with another." Confession of sin on the part of the saint means therefore to say the same thing that God does about that sin, to agree with God as to all the implication of that sin as it relates to the Christian who commits it and to a holy God against whom it is committed.[4]

The verb *confess* is in the present tense, which emphasizes continuous action. This does not mean a Christian is to confess continually the same sin, but rather that confession is a continuous action if sin is present. The popular idea that confession should be made while praying during one's quiet time is sure to cause problems in the spiritual life. Confession could take place at that time, but the best time for confession is immediately after sin comes into one's life. The idea of setting aside only one time during the day for communicating with God will perhaps do more to perpetuate carnality than any one thing. The reason for this is that a Christian is commanded to *pray without ceasing*. A Christian should have daily Bible study and prayer. He should not substitute this with reading a verse of Scripture, a cute thought, or inspiring poem and think this type of spiritual rabbit's foot will guarantee a proper spiritual life.

Confession of sins is not the complete answer to spiritual maturity. Ideally it is better if sin is never allowed to enter to break fellowship.

The Spiritually Maturing Christian

Rather than giving an exact definition of spiritual maturity, the Scriptures describe the one who is mature. There are two terms involved: τέλείοις and πνευματικός. The word τέλείοις means *completeness (them that are perfect,* 1 Corinthians 2:6); in the context, the term refers to those who can comprehend the wisdom of God—the particular wisdom that was a mystery until Paul the steward revealed it. Vincent, commenting on 1 Corinthians 2:6, says it is:

> Paul's term for matured Christians. See Ephesians iv. 13, where a *perfect* (τέλειον) *man* is contrasted with children (νήπιοι, ver. 14). So 1 Corinthians xiv. 20: "In malice *children,* in understanding *men* (lit., perfect.)"[5]

Wuest comments:

> Paul writes the Corinthians that he speaks wisdom among those who are perfect (1 Corinthians 2:6), and uses *teleios*. But he says that he could not speak to them as to spiritual Christians, but as to carnal ones, namely, babes in Christ (1 Corinthians 3:1). In passing, it might be well to note that the phrase "babes in Christ" as Paul uses it in the Greek, does not mean "young converts," but "Christians who have not attained to a mature Christian experience."[6]

The word τέλειοι is used in Philippians 3:15[7] regarding those who, with Paul, are stretching forth to the prize of the calling of God. In other words, the word τέλειοι refers to Christians who are in a mental state to be thinking on things above. They are ordering their lives here on earth with eternity's values in view, which is a definite mark of spiritual maturity.

In Hebrews 5:14, the Bible describes a mature Christian as *them that are of full age*. The words *full age* translate the word τελείων. The full-aged Christian is marked by two things. First, he is capable of handling the meat of the Word. In context, this refers to deeper teachings about Christ in His Melchizedek priesthood. Second, the full-aged Christian is set apart by the fact that he is discerning (*to discern both good and evil*). He can discern because his spiritual faculties have been exercised (γεγυμνασμένα).

This rules out the new Christian, for his spiritual senses have yet to be fully tried. The young Christian is not noted for his discerning ability; even the converse is true as 1 Timothy 3:6, points out, for the novice readily falls into the temptations of the devil:

Not a novice, lest being lifted up with pride he fall into the condemnation of the devil.

The second term that describes a mature Christian is *spiritual*. The word *spiritual*, as used in Scripture, means more than being properly related to the Holy Spirit. The word πνευμτικός is used four times in the Church Epistles as it relates individuals to this characteristic. First Corinthians 2:15 says:

But he that is spiritual judgeth all things, yet he himself is judged of no man.

Here the note of discernment, ἀνακρίνει, is struck in the first occurrence of the word. The word πνευματικός is here used as a synonym for τελείοις, found in verse six. The apostle used πνευματικός to show that the ones who are complete (τελείοις) are geared toward understanding the spiritual things he had for them through the mysteries.

The word *spiritual* is used the second time in 1 Corinthians 3:1, in contrast to the carnal Christian. The respective diets are contrasted in verse two:

I have fed you with milk, and not with meat...

Recall now that one of the characteristics of a mature Christian in Hebrews 5:14 was his ability to handle the solid food of the Word:

But strong meat belongeth to them that are of full age...

Also, the one who used milk was a babe (νήπιος), the same as in 1 Corinthians 3:1.

And I, brethren, could not speak unto you as unto spiritual, but as unto carnal, even as unto babes in Christ.

The word πλευματικός occurs again in 1 Corinthians 14:37:

If any man think himself to be a prophet, or spiritual, let him acknowledge that the things that I write unto you are the commandments of the Lord.

The context of 1 Corinthians 14 is order in the local church in reference to speaking in tongues and prophesying. Paul had just commented on the prohibition of women speaking in the assembly. To reinforce his statements, he says in effect:

If you want a test of your spirituality, see if you will recognize the things I say as the commands of the Lord.

A spiritual person, then, is one who knows fully and experientially (ἐπιγινωσκέτω) the things Paul writes. The Christian who is characterized by πνευματικός fully realizes the Lordship of the Word of God over his life. It is obvious by the matriarchal orientation of Bible-believing Sunday schools today that a low watermark of true spirituality exists. Allowing the Lordship of the Word in one's life is not a characteristic of a new convert.

The last appearance of πνευματικός, in reference to the spiritual condition of a believer, is in Galatians 6:1:

Brethren, if a man be overtaken in a fault, ye which are spiritual, restore such an one in the spirit of meekness; considering thyself, lest thou also be tempted.

The one who needs restoration is involved in a fault—that is, a trespass. Precisely, trespass is not a sin, for sin requires knowledge.[8] Παραπτώματι is an unrighteous act or thought without knowledge that it is wrong. Robertson says it means, "literally, a falling aside, a slip or lapse in the papyri rather than a willful sin."[9] This is the time for restoration. People are more apt to respond to correction while in a state of trespass. When the trespass reaches the point of willful, knowledgeable sin, the sinning party will resent an approach by a spiritual man.

The nature of this type of ministry would seem to rule out a new believer. It is only normal for a new Christian to not have a working and balanced knowledge of Scripture whereby he could determine what is sin and what is not. Even more difficult is the ability to detect when someone is in a state of trespass. This takes real discernment, something on the nature of 1 Corinthians 2:5[10] and Hebrews 5:14.[11] A new convert, in fact, is usually the one who would be in a trespass because of his lack of knowledge of the Word.

It appears valid to understand that a mature Christian has the following characteristics:

1. He has had his spiritual faculties exercised (Hebrews 5:14).
2. He has had his faith tried (James 1:3, 4).
3. He has room for spiritual progress (Philippians 2:12).
4. He is a complete man spiritually (Ephesians 4:13).
5. He is full-grown in mind (1 Corinthians 14:20).
6. He can handle the meat of the Word (Hebrews 5:14).
7. He recognizes the Lordship of the Word of God (1 Corinthians 14:3).
8. He is in a position to restore others (Galatians 6:1).

9. He can appreciate dispensationalism (1 Corinthians 2:6, 7).
10. He is contrasted with a carnal Christian (1 Corinthians 3:1).
11. He discerns all things (1 Corinthians 2:15).
12. He is discerned by no man (1 Corinthians 2:15).

Spiritual maturity, as Paul states in Philippians 2:12, is somewhat relative. There is always room for growth. The older a Christian is, the more mature he should be. It is sad to see older Christians who become silly in their later years and consequently lose the confidence of younger men. Somewhere they stopped growing and began coasting.

The time it takes for a new believer to become mature varies from person to person and is directly proportional to his knowledge of the Word of God, understanding of his enemies, and opportunity to exercise his spiritual faculties and have victory over temptation.

THE NEED FOR TEMPTATION

John Bunyan once said, "Temptation provokes me to look upward to God."[12] Temptation was certainly meant for the benefit and strengthening of believers. One of the reasons God did not drive out the enemies of the land of Canaan was that the children of Israel needed to learn how to trust. Temptation likewise is a solicitation to do evil, but God allows it as an opportunity for spiritual growth.

One of the reasons God leaves Christians here on earth after they are saved is so they can grow and become more Christ-like. To accomplish this growth, He allows forces that are diametrically opposed to everything the Christian would try to do for God. Hebrews 5:14 speaks of the result of this conflict:

But strong meat belongeth to them that are of full age, even those who by reason of use have their senses exercised to discern both good and evil.

The reason for their being *full age* (τελείων) or mature was that they were presently in a condition of having their senses exercised.

The word *senses* is αἰσθητήρια, which is used only here in the New Testament. It is used in the Septuagint of Jeremiah in 4:19, where the Hebrew word is קיר—which is translated by most as *wall*.[13] The Authorized Version says, *I am pained at my very heart*. Literally, it is the *walls of my heart*.[14] This is a metaphorical term that shows the intensity of pain Jeremiah felt in a spiritual sense. Thus:

The αἰσθητήρια are the organs which are capable of, or at least susceptible to, discrimination between good and evil, the τέλειος having so trained them by exercise that they have become a corresponding habitus.[15]

This immaterial part of a Christian must have the privilege of being exercised before the person can become a mature

Christian. The result is the ability to discern between good, or fitting, and evil, or things lacking.

A Christian should look forward to temptation, for he knows first that:

There hath no temptation taken you but such as is common to man: but God is faithful, who will not suffer you to be tempted above that ye are able; but will with the temptation also make a way to escape, that ye may be able to bear it. (1 Corinthians 10:13).

Secondly, he is to count it all joy to have temptations, for this leads to maturity and the crown of life (James 1:4, 12). James says a believer is to *count it all joy* when temptation comes because he knows experientially that these trials work patience, and patience brought to completion in the life of a Christian brings spiritual maturity (James 1:2-4). James introduces a synonym for maturity—*entire* (ὁλόκληροι). It is translated *whole* in 1 Thessalonians 5:23. It is used in the Septuagint in Leviticus 23:5 of *seven full weeks*. The Christian then can only be in this state of *lacking nothing* when he has had victory over temptation. Temptation is not something to be feared and dreaded, but rightfully considered as a true stepping stone to maturity and future reward.

Happy is he who comes through temptation victorious, because he gets the crown of life (James 1:12). The Christian should be well-informed of the fact that how well he comes through temptations is a test of his love for the Lord. This is another reason why he should know his enemies well.

THE NEED FOR TIME

The very concept of the word mature involves time. One thinks immediately of age or growth. Returning to Hebrews 5:14, notice the word exercised (γεγυμνασμένα). This perfect participle shows that the mature or full-aged Christians were in a state of exercising their discerning abilities. Time is required for this exercising.

Hebrews 5:14 states, *who by reason of use* (τῶν διὰ τὴν ἕξιν). The word *use* is ἕξιν, which indicates time is required. Westcott says:

> ξιν (here only in N.T.) expresses not the process but the result, the condition which has been *produced by past exercise*....[16]

The writer of the book of Hebrews plainly states that *because of the time* (διὰτὸνχρόνον) they should have been teachers. It is true that being a teacher is not identical with maturity, but the writer links the terms in the context of spiritual maturity, which indicates that to function best in the sphere of one›s spiritual gift requires maturity.

A man chosen for the function of overseer (bishop) should surely be a spiritually mature Christian in order to meet the requirements and descriptions in the Word of God (Acts 20:28;

1 Timothy 3:1-7; Titus 1:6-9; 1 Peter 5:2-4). An overseer, at the same time, is not to be a recent convert or novice. The word *novice* is νεόφυτον, coming from νεος, which means new in time, and φυω, *to spring up*.[17] The reason he cannot be chosen for this function is because he has not been able to have consistent victory over the Satanic temptation of pride. The Scriptures link his qualifications, among other things, to one of his enemies and his apparent failure to apply the proper defense. This new convert needs time to mature. The new convert must have his faith approved to work endurance; endurance brought to completion equals maturity and qualifications (James 1:3, 4).

THE NEED FOR THE WORD OF GOD

Thy word have I hid in mine heart, that I might not sin against thee. (Psalm 119:11).

The Scriptures are profitable to equip the man of God for every good work (2 Timothy 3:16, 17). The Word of God is the nourishment to help a believer grow with respect to salvation (1 Peter 2:2). Hebrews 5:14 indicates that one's inability to handle the word of righteousness is a sign of spiritual decline. The solid food is for the mature. A Christian is not expected to stay in one place in reference to the knowledge and practice of the Word of God; he is to advance.

The road to spiritual maturity is paved with the Word of God. The growing Christians of whom John writes in 1 John 2:14 were strong (ἰσχυροί). The reason they were strong was because the Word of God was abiding in them and they had victory over Satanic temptations (1 John 2:4).

> The word of God, residing in their hearts in an unhindered, welcome state, was that which, together with the power of the Holy Spirit, gave these young men victory over Satan, the Pernicious One, who sought to drag them down with himself into the ruin that someday will be his.[18]

Keeping or guarding the Word of God is considered the test of the love of God being brought to its fullest extent in a Christian's life (1 John 2:5). The fruit of the Spirit—love—can be perfected, but it requires tenacious guarding of the Word of God. This refers to those who show maturity with respect to love.

When one is grounded in the Word regarding the content of salvation he has in Christ, he is able to stand against the philosophies of the world (Colossians 2:7, 8). In fact, the purpose for teaching the Word of God is to:

> ...*present every man perfect ($τέλειον$ or mature) in Christ Jesus. (Colossians 1: 28).*

When a person becomes mature in Christ because of his ability gained in spiritual conflict, he begins to realize the simplicity of Biblical Christianity and becomes less enchanted with the many trappings of formal Protestantism. It must be realized that he will be misunderstood, like Hannah of old when she prayed for Samuel or the spiritual man in 1 Corinthians 2:15 who went undiscerned. His suggestions to those held captive in legalism or Galatianism "seems to be a suggestion toward 'backsliding,' and no zealously minded person will easily choose such a course."[19] His voice will be like one crying in the wilderness, but for the sake of the Word of God and the life of the church, he must speak the truth in love. The effect of spiritual maturity will show itself in many different ways. Certain Biblical concepts will begin to have new meanings that were unappreciated and lay dormant.

The concepts set forth in the subsequent chapter may seem to many as hard sayings, but the ideas are true to the mature Christian's experience. Even more importantly, they are in concord with the Word of God.

Endnotes

1. C.I. Scofield, *Plain Papers on the Doctrine of the Holy Spirit* (Grand Rapids. Michigan: Baker Book House, 1966), p. 58.
2. Kenneth S. Wuest, *Golden Nuggets From the Greek New Testament* (Grand Rapids: Wm. B. Eerdmans Publishing Co., 1940), pp. 33-34.
3. *But without faith it is impossible to please him: for he that cometh to God must believe that he is, and that he is a rewarder of them that diligently seek him. (Hebrews 11:6).*
4. Kenneth S. Wuest, *In These Last Days* (Grand Rapids: Wm. B. Eerdmans Publishing Co., 1964), p. 104.
5. Marvin R. Vincent, *Word Studies in the New Testament*, III (Grand Rapids: Wm. B. Eerdmans Publishing Co., 1946), p. 195.
6. Kenneth S. Wuest, *Treasures from the Greek New Testament* (Grand Rapids: Wm. B. Eerdmans Publishing Co., 1941), pp. 114-15.
7. *Let us therefore, as many as be perfect, be thus minded… (Philippians 3:15).*
8. See section where sin is defined, p. 171.
9. A. T. Robertson, *Word Pictures in the New Testament*, IV (Nashville: Broadman Press, 1931), 315.
10. *That your faith should not stand in the wisdom of men, but in the power of God. (1 Corinthians 2:5).*
11. *But strong meat belongeth to them that are of full age, even those who by reason of use have their senses exercised to discern both good and evil. (Hebrews 5:14).*
12. Frank S. Mead (ed.), *Encyclopedia of Religious Quotations* (London: Peter Davies, 1965), p. 437.

13 *The Englishman's Hebrew and Chaldee Concordance of the Old Testament* (Grand Rapids: Zondervan Publishing House, 1970), p. 1108.
14 Francis Brown, S. R. Driver, and Charles A. Briggs, *A Hebrew and English Lexicon of the Old Testament* (Oxford: Clarendon Press, 1907), p. 885.
15 Gerhard Kittel (ed.), *Theological Dictionary of the New Testament*, I (Grand Rapids: Wm. B. Eerdmans Publishing Co., 1964), 188.
16 Brooke Foss Westcott, *The Epistle to the Hebrews* (Grand Rapids: Wm. B. Eerdmans Publishing Co., 1970), p. 135.
17 Kenneth S. Wuest, *The Pastoral Epistles in the Greek New Testament* (Grand Rapids: Wm. B. Eerdmans Publishing Co., 1952), p. 58.
18 Wuest, *In*, p. 125.
19 Lewis Sperry Chafer, *He That Is Spiritual* (Grand Rapids: Dunham Publishing Co., 1964), p. 131.

CHAPTER 5

THE EFFECT OF SPIRITUAL MATURITY

...to approach the subject with an unprejudiced mind and to be concerned only with what the Bible actually teaches.

Lewis Sperry Chafer

The Realization of the Simplicity of the Christian Life

Upon entering a church at the time of worship hour on Sunday morning, it would be difficult to detect that Christian life and fellowship with God are simple. A visitor would be quite aware of the ups and downs, the extended preliminaries, the long pulpit prayers, the general atmosphere of a conditioned response, and a sacred cow program steamrolling its way along. A person not culturally conditioned before salvation might find it hard to get in step with the proper and accepted manipulations, which are called oddly enough "worship services."

The idea of coming to a place for the *purpose* of worshipping is an Old Testament concept. It was acceptable in the Old Testament because God the Son dwelt in the temple in Jerusalem. The simplicity of Christian life was prophetically set forth in the account of the woman at the well in the Gospel of John, Chapter 4.

> *The woman saith unto him, Sir, I perceive that thou art a prophet.[20] Our fathers worshipped in this mountain; and ye say, that in Jerusalem is the place where men ought to worship.[21] Jesus saith unto her, Woman, believe me, the hour cometh, when ye shall neither in this mountain, nor yet at Jerusalem, worship the Father.[22] Ye worship ye know not what: we know what we worship: for salvation is of the Jews.[23] But the hour cometh, and now is, when the true worshippers shall worship the Father in spirit and in truth: for the Father seeketh such to worship him.[24] God is a Spirit: and they that worship him must worship him in spirit and truth. (John 4:19-24).*

The woman, having a theological bias, thought it good to worship at Mount Gerizim. The Lord Jesus made her aware that true worship was a spiritual thing and was not at this time—and more specifically, in the future—limited to a geographic location. Following this principle, the early church never came together for the purpose of worshipping. They came together for the purpose of breaking bread, praying, ministering the Word, and exhortation (Acts 2:42; Hebrews 10:25; Acts 20:7). No doubt worship took place, but they did not meet for that purpose.

The average church service (so-called) today is cluttered with a mixture of Judaism and Roman Catholic theology, with a Protestant veneer and traditions for emotional acceptance. The Apostle Paul said:

Neither is [God] worshipped with men's hands, as though he needed anything, seeing he giveth to all life, and breath, and all things. (Acts 17:25).

The point he is making is, of course, in reference to idols as an approach to God. The principle is this: There is nothing man can make (neither wood nor worship services) that will help in an effort to worship and have fellowship with God. True worship is controlled by the mind, not helped along by man's esthetic nature (Romans 12:1, 2; John 4:19-24; Ephesians 4:23). The simplicity of Christian life, then, is merely being Biblically related to the Spirit of God and being led by Him moment by moment (Colossians 3:17; John 15:4, 5). The mature Christian will be more concerned with searching the Scriptures than merely accepting tradition.

The words of C. H. Mackintosh are appropriate at this point:

And let it be carefully noted that we will listen to nothing on this subject but the voice of Holy Scripture.

> Let not reason speak, for we own it not. Let not tradition lift her voice, for we wholly disregard her. Let not expediency thrust itself upon us, for we shall give it no place whatever.

Along the same line, he wrote:

> If we admit, for a moment, that, in some things, we must have recourse to tradition and expediency, then who will undertake to fix the boundary line? If it be allowable to depart from Scripture at all, how far are we to go? If the authority of tradition be admitted at all, who is to fix its domain?[1]

Not only is the simplicity of Christian life seen in the assembly, but also in the personal spiritual life of the Spirit-led believer. True spiritual service will be covered later, but it is necessary first to consider the spiritual attitude of a Christian. Ephesians 1:12 says the Christian has been predestinated for the purpose (εἰς τὸ εἶναι) of living to the praise and glory of God. Only a Spirit-led Christian can fulfill this determination of God. He brings glory to God in whatever he does or does not do, if directed by the Holy Spirit. Chafer pointed out:

> If it is His will for us, we are just as spiritual when resting, playing, ill or infirm as when we are active in service.[2]

The maturing Christian is led by the Spirit (Romans 6:14). The maturing Christian is satisfied in believing the Holy Spirit will lead him to fulfill the Biblical imperatives bearing upon his life, without setting up an extra written or unwritten code of conduct (Galatians 5:18, 23; Romans 8:3, 4). The simplicity of Christian life sets one free of superstitious devotions. Often it is declared, "I just don't feel right unless I spend time with God in the early morning." Whether a person feels right is rather irrelevant, for the maturing Christian realizes he spends every moment of the day with God—not just the early hours—and depends on Him moment by moment. Bible study should never be degraded to being a fix to remove spiritual problems. Unfortunately, many people come to depend solely on their daily five-minute energizers, not realizing their spiritual enemies feed upon this anemic type of spiritual mentality. The Word says:

Study [or bend every effort] to shew thyself approved unto God, a workman that needeth not to be ashamed, rightly dividing the word of truth. (2 Timothy 2: 15).

When a Christian begins to realize the simple aspect of Christian life, he understands grace.

AN UNDERSTANDING OF GRACE

The Bible very clearly reveals that a Christian is not under law, but under grace. Romans 6:15 states:

What then? shall we sin, because we are not under the law, but under grace? God forbid.

The fact that a believer is under grace is a settled question—but what is grace? Grace is easier to describe than define. The Greek word is used in the New Testament at least 156 times and is translated by eleven different words. Chafer says:

> The meaning of the word grace, as used in the New Testament, is not unlike its meaning as employed in common speech—but for one important exception, namely, in the Bible the word often represents that which is limitless, since it represents realities which are infinite and eternal. It is nothing less than the unlimited love of God expressing itself in measureless grace.[3]

God forgives without striking a blow to the sinner. The Father forsook His unique Son (Matt. 27:46) for lost humanity. This grace is an attitude of Christ whereby He, though rich, was willing to become poor so believing sinners might be rich through Him (2 Corinthians 8:9).

While living in a carnal state, a believer will not appreciate grace; it will not interest him, for he seeks out law principles as guidelines. It was grace (χάρις) that Paul realized had delivered him from a carnal state (Romans 7:25). An immature Christian never gets past the idea that he is saved by grace (Hebrews 6:1, 2). As one matures, he becomes aware that Christian life is by grace as well (Romans 7:25). A mature Christian will confess that:

> It is often the "beginning of days" in a Christian's life when he really believes and heeds the Word of God enough to be made aware of his own limitations, and seriously considers the exact revelation as to what he of himself can or cannot do, and what the Spirit who indwells him has come to do.[4]

The mature Christian realizes that adhering to a law principle to promote righteousness is to fall from grace (Galatians 5:4). As a believer grows in grace, he becomes more and more aware of his new content of faith in this dispensation (Ephesians 3:2-20).

AN UNDERSTANDING OF DISPENSATIONALISM

When one speaks of Christian life, he has—by the term "Christian"—limited himself in the application of Scripture for his rule of life. All the Bible is authoritative for faith (that means it is to be believed), but all the Scriptures are not authoritative for practice. Understanding the dispensational (the word *dispensation* means "House Rules") factor in Christian life simply means one has recognized that to be pleasing to God, he must submit to the content of faith that God meant for him in this dispensation. He is not to regulate his life by the content of faith and salvation (for example, of the Old Testament economy).

Nothing will help Christian life more than knowing how to properly interpret Scripture. We cannot practice our Christian life by following what a Christian denomination believes. We must follow what the Bible actually teaches. It should be carefully noted that the church (the Body of Christ) is called a mystery. It was never reveled in the Scriptures before the book of Acts. Matthew 16:18, according to this context, is talking about an assembly that Christ will build in the millennial kingdom, not the group of today. It is always very wrong to mix dispensations. This is a truth the "pre-wrath Rapture" folks need to understand.

In Galatians 5:18, Paul makes it very clear that in this dispensation a Christian is not under any law principle:

But if ye be led of the Spirit, ye are not under the law.

When ending the list of the fruit of the Spirit, he says:

...against such there is no law. (Galatians 5:23).

Any believer who puts himself under a law principle is in for a real struggle in his spiritual life—a struggle that can end only in certain failure. The reason is that the law was never given to bring about righteousness before God. Chafer points out:

After declaring that the law has passed, either as the grounds of the justification of the sinner (Galatians 3:24), or as the rule of life for the believer (Galatians 3:25), the Apostle challenges the law-ridden Christians at Galatia to consider the fact and force of two great covenants which can in no wise co-exist.[5]

Christians are heirs according to *promise*, not according to *law*.

And if ye be Christ's, then are ye Abraham's seed, and heirs according to the promise. (Galatians 3:29).

The law showed the sinner the sinfulness of his sin and the power of the sin principle within himself (Romans 7:8, 13; Galatians 3:19).

The Christian must realize what it means to be under grace. This understanding, in its fullness, will never be adequately appreciated experientially until one has a working knowledge of his spiritual enemies. Paul shows that the *wisdom of God in a mystery* (1 Corinthians 2:7) is best taught *among them that are perfect* (τοῖς τελείοις) or mature. This particular wisdom was not revealed in the Old Testament, but now was made manifest. The apostle could not completely fulfill his stewardship in the Corinthian church because they were carnal (1 Corinthians 3:1, 4). They could not stand the meat of this heavenly wisdom:

I have fed you with milk and not with meat. (1 Corinthians 3:2).

An adequate understanding and appreciation of dispensationalism is most necessary to true Christian service.

The Realization of True Spiritual Service

Any service other than that which was foreordained for the individual, though valuable in itself, cannot be called "good works" because it is not the personal outworking of the will of God. The discovery and realization of "good works" is not experienced by all believers, but only by those who have presented their bodies a living sacrifice, holy, acceptable unto God; who are not "conformed to this world," but are "transformed" (transfigured) by the renewing of their minds (Romans 12:1, 2).[6]

It has become a popular pastime in many Christian circles to "do anything for Jesus," to be busy ("Better to burn out than to rust out."). One hears this often when a Christian is not Scripturally commanded to do either. It is possible to be zealous but be wrong (Philippians 3:6). The spiritually maturing Christian will realize there are certain works he should do that are called good. Ephesians 2:10 states:

For we are his workmanship, created in Christ Jesus unto good works, which God hath before ordained that we should walk in them.

This verse must be examined more closely. A Christian is presented as a result of God's doing (ποίημα). The μα ending emphasizes the result of God's action.[7] The action spoken of is the baptizing work of the Holy Spirit, because the believer was created in Christ Jesus (Ephesians 2:15; 4:24; 2 Corinthians 5:17; Galatians 6:15; Colossians 3:10). Now, being God's product, the Christian is set unto good works (ἐπὶ ἔργοις ἀγαθοῖς). This is his new position in Christ.

These good works are of a unique type, described as those *which God hath before ordained*. *Ordained* is προητοίμασεν, which means that God at a point in eternity past prepared definite works for each individual Christian to do. For this reason, Spirit-led believers should order their lives in the sphere of these previously prepared works (ἵνα ἐν αὐτοῖς περιπατήσωμεν). Literally, this is *in order that in them we should walk*.

This present evil age says, "Do your own thing." But God says, "Do what I have prepared." This requirement constitutes the rules of true Christian service. Unless a Christian abides by them, he will not be rewarded.

…if a man also strive for masteries, yet is he not crowned, except he strive lawfully. (2 Timothy 2:5).

Works done outside faith are sin (Romans 14:23) and are worthless (φαῦλον; 2 Corinthians 5:10). They will no doubt comprise that which is burned (1 Corinthians 3:15).

THE PRIESTHOOD OF THE BELIEVER

The practical application of the priesthood of the believer is a truth enjoyed by the maturing Christian. Since the Lord Jesus Christ opened the way for all (Matt. 27:51), all believers since Pentecost have become priests. Christians are a:

> ... *holy priesthood, to offer up spiritual sacrifices, acceptable to God by Jesus Christ. (1 Peter 2:5).*

Peter again states:

> *But ye are a chosen generation, a royal priesthood... (1 Peter 2:9).*

Part of a Christian's true spiritual service is to offer up unbloody or spiritual sacrifices. These sacrifices constitute an acceptable service unto God. Some have seen in the sacrifices the areas of the person, purse, and praise. A Christian is to offer his body as a *living sacrifice* unto God (Romans 12:1). This sacrifice relates specifically to the operation of his spiritual gift, as Romans 12:3-8 indicates. A growing Christian who is having victory over his enemies is in a position to offer his body, so the Holy Spirit may manifest Himself through him (1 Corinthians 12:7).

A mature Christian will put away the lower, beggarly elements of the law—such as tithing—and come to realize he now gives as a priest of God. His giving is a spiritual sacrifice:

> *But to do good and to communicate forget not: for with such sacrifices God is well pleased. (Hebrews 13:16).*

The word *communicate* is κοινωνίας, which is used often in the New Testament for Christian giving (2 Corinthians 9:13; Galatians 6:6; Philippians 4:14).[8]

Christian giving is not for the purpose of piling up funds for empire building, but to meet the needs of God's people:

> *For even in Thessalonica ye sent once and again unto my necessity. (Philippians 4:16).*

> *But I have all, and abound: I am full. having received of Epaphroditus the things which were sent from you, an odor of a sweet smell, a sacrifice acceptable, wellpleasing to God. (Philippians 4:18).*

Another channel of true spiritual service is praise to God. Hebrews 13:15 states:

> *By him therefore let us offer the sacrifice of praise to God continually, that is the fruit of our lips giving thanks to his name.*

Praise is the fruit of the lips. It is confessing to His name or confessing all that Christ is. This is illustrated by Hosea 14:2:

Take with you words, and return unto Jehovah: say unto him, Take away all iniquity, and accept that which is good: so will we render as bullocks the offering of our lips. (American Standard Version).

This attitude of heart enables the Holy Spirit to work through a Christian to the glory of God.

THE PROPER USE OF SPIRITUAL GIFTS

First Corinthians 12:7 states:

But the manifestation of the Spirit is given to every man to profit withal.

The following could be summarized about spiritual gifts:

1. They are a manifestation of the Spirit for service (1 Corinthians 12:7).
2. They are sovereignly given (Hebrews 2:4; 1 Corinthians 12:28).
3. They are not natural, developed talents (1 Corinthians 12:12, 13).
4. There are no true Christians without a spiritual gift (1 Corinthians 12:7; 1 Peter 4:10).

5. They determine the priorities in a Christian's service (Romans 12:4-8).
6. They are not all permanent (1 Corinthians 13:8-13).
7. They are to be exercised in love (1 Corinthians 13:1-13).

The appropriate use of spiritual gifts could eliminate some of the contemporary problems in church planting. One problem is financial barriers. There is a popular saying today about a mission church becoming self-supporting. This usually means it is financially situated so it can operate like a big city church. The local church in the New Testament knew nothing of this self-supporting concept, because these churches operated on the basis of spiritual gifts; the ministry of the Word depended on spiritually gifted men (Ephesians 4:11, 12). Every member was in full-time Christian service. The early church was not terribly hampered by the self-supporting problem, because they knew spiritual progress was not dependent on a beautiful edifice, large property holdings, and a huge staff of paid personnel. Today—according to convention and association magazines—when a pastor leaves a church for other service, his success is usually measured by bricks and mortar rather than the quality of mature and equipped saints.

Part of being a healthy Christian is realizing that each one has a gift as a member of the body of Christ, then to function properly in love so the body does not suffer (1 Corinthians 12:26, 27). Spiritual gifts can be misused, as is evident by 1 Corinthians 12-14. Proper use of spiritual gifts requires spiritual maturity to see the church has no division and the Word of God is obeyed regarding the utterance gifts (1 Corinthians 12:24-26; 14:33-36; 1 Thessalonians 5:19; 1 Timothy 2:11, 12). When a spiritual Christian finds his niche in God's plan for service, he will begin to realize his true witness for Christ.

THE SCRIPTURAL TYPE OF WITNESS

You are writing a Gospel,
A chapter a day.
Men read what you write,
Whether faithless or true, Say!
What is the Gospel according to you?

Paul B. Gilbert

To answer such a question could prove incriminating to many, but it should be answered to see if orthopraxy equals orthodoxy.

The basic meaning of the word *witness* refers primarily to life. It is a life that represents the truth of the Word of God, even if it requires death.[9] It is interesting to note that those who enter death for their testimony are called *true* or *faithful* witnesses (Revelation 1:5, 2:13, 3:14, 17:16; John 18:37). They were faithfully living their lives to the end. The heroes of faith in Hebrews 11 were good witnesses because their actions were brought about by faith (Hebrews 11:4, 5, 12:1).

The unsaved would more likely be brought under conviction of the Holy Spirit if the life and lip of the witnessing Christian were coincident. The success of the Gospel at Thessalonica illustrates this:

For our gospel came not unto you in word only, but also in power, and in the Holy Ghost, and in much assurance; as ye know what manner of men we were among you for your sake. (1 Thessalonians 1:5).

Similarly, a mature Christian will be a good witness. One major idea in maturity is the believer's ability to apply the Word of God to himself so his life radiates the graces of the Lord Jesus Christ; thus, the Gospel in life complements the Gospel in word.

Endnotes

1. C.H. Mackintosh, *The Assembly of God*, III (Neptune, New Jersey: Loizeaux Brothers, 1898), 13-14.
2. Lewis Sperry Chafer, *He That Is Spiritual* (Grand Rapids: Dunham Publishing Co., 1954), p. 59.
3. Lewis Sperry Chafer, *Grace* (Grand Rapids: Zondervan Publishing House, 1922), p. 3.
4. Chafer, *He*, p. 120.
5. Chafer, *Grace*, p. 188.
6. Chafer, *He*, pp. 55-56.
7. Bruce M. Metzger, *Lexical Aids for Students of New Testament Greek* (Princeton, New Jersey: By the author, 1965), p. 55.
8. Archibald Thomas Robertson, *Word Pictures in the New Testament*, V (Nashville: Broadman Press, 1932), 449.
9. Gerhard Kittel (ed.), *Theological Dictionary of the New Testament*, IV (Grand Rapids: Wm. B. Eerdmans Publishing Co., 1967), 495.

CONCLUSION

"I would be a spiritual giant if I did not have to get up in the morning!"

A Christian once said this in a joking manner. The tragic part of such a story is the fact that many Christians are committed to this unscriptural creed, which is no joke at all. For some defeated Christians, their only consistent testimony occurs when they are sleeping. This oscillating characteristic is due to their inability to handle their spiritual enemies, which are the only roadblocks to proper and healthy spirituality.

This book concerned itself in large measure with the enemy within—the flesh. The carnal Christian lives his life in the realm of the flesh and its strong desires. He is controlled only by sources other than the Holy Spirit. The carnal Christian can never be joyous because the lusts of the flesh war against the soul (1 Peter 2:11). The main idea that was stressed, however, was supernatural control for the flesh or sin principle. The believer who learns to walk by the Spirit will not have to live with the guilt that surrounds the works of the flesh when they are brought to completion (Galatians 5:16-21).

The Spirit-filled Christian is the prime target for Satanic and worldly temptations. In fact, *only* a Spirit-controlled Christian who is experiencing a measure of victory in his life can be tempted. A carnal Christian is not tempted by the devil or the world, for he is already drawn away from the Spirit's control. One must be on a higher level to be brought down to a lower plane. The Spirit-walking Christian must be sober to recognize the enemies when they tempt him.

The child of God must learn to use his defenses. He must learn when to reckon, when to stand, and when and how to direct his love. The conflict can be handled by any Christian, if only he uses what God has provided. The more mature the believer becomes, the subtler the temptations become. The maturing saint is to stand against Satan while properly using the mental or spiritual armor given to him by the Lord. The temptations coming from Satan will never appear as they really are. Therefore, a Christian must be very discerning to detect the enemy and the specific temptation.

The maturing Christian is always a candidate for temptations from the world. The mature believer is one who is led of the Spirit (Romans 8:14) and therefore has love being produced in his life. He becomes responsible for directing this love properly. If he directs it at the world, he cannot at the same time direct it to his Heavenly Father and the brethren. Becoming entangled in the world is a snare from which it is difficult to be freed.

James points out very clearly that the way a believer becomes a mature Christian is by having victory over temptation (James 1:2-4). Temptation can only have its source in the three enemies that have been mentioned. Therefore, before a Christian can become mature, he must be able—by the Lord's grace—to know his enemies and the Scriptural defense for every temptation of each enemy. This is why a Christian's spiritual enemies are so closely related to spiritual maturity.

As a believer learns more about his enemies and the proper defense against each, he will begin to grow spiritually and live a more consistent life that is pleasing to God and the brethren. The results of the mature life are far-reaching and extend into every aspect of the Christian's personal life, ministry, and future rewards. The mature Christian is on the road to spiritual joy and spiritual prosperity simply because he took seriously God's grace in providing victory over our spiritual enemies—the world, the flesh, and the devil.

BIBLIOGRAPHY

A. TEXTS AND VERSIONS

The American Standard Version. New York: Thomas Nelson & Sons, 1901.

King James Version. New York: American Bible Society, 1816.

B. GRAMMARS AND LEXICONS

Abbott-Smith, G. *A Manual Greek Lexicon of the New Testament.* Edinburgh: T. & T. Clark, 1921. Pp. xv+512.

Arndt, William F., and F. Wilbur Gingrich. *A Greek-English Lexicon of the New Testament and Other Early Christian Literature.* Cambridge: The University Press, 1957. Pp. xxxvii+909.

Blass, F., and A. Debrunner. *A Greek Grammar of the New Testament and Other Early Christian Literature.* Chicago and London: The University of Chicago Press, 1961. Pp. xxxvii+325.

Brown, Francis, S.R. Driver, and Charles A. Briggs. *A Hebrew and English Lexicon of the Old Testament.* With an appendix containing the Biblical Aramaic. Based on the lexicon of William Gesenius as translated by Edward Robinson. London: Oxford University Press, 1952. Pp. 1126.

Dana, H.E., and Julius R. Mantey. *A Manual of Grammar of the Greek New Testament.* New York: The Macmillan Co., 1927. Pp. xvi+368.

The Englishman's Hebrew and Chaldee Concordance of the Old Testament. Grand Rapids: Zondervan Publishing House, 1970.

Gillespie, G.K. *The Englishman's Greek Concordance of the New Testament.* London: Samuel Bagster & Sons, Ltd., 1903. Pp. xxxv+1020Lxxi.

Goetchius, Eugene Van Ness. *The Language of the New Testament.* New York: Charles Scribner's Sons, 1965. Pp. xvii+349.

Kittel, Gerhard (ed.). *Theological Dictionary of the New Testament*. 5 vols. Grand Rapids: Wm. B. Eerdmans Publishing Co., 1964-65, 1967.

Liddell, Henry George, and Robert Scott. *A Greek-English Lexicon*. Oxford: The Clarendon Press, 1843. Pp. xlv+2042.

Metzger, Bruce M. *Lexical Aids for Students of New Testament Greek*. Princeton, New Jersey: By the author, 1965. Pp. ix+118.

Moule, C.F.D. *An Idiom Book of New Testament Greek*. Cambridge: The University Press, 1953. Pp. x+246.

Moulton, James Hope, and George Milligan. *The Vocabulary of the Greek Testament*. Grand Rapids: Wm. B. Eerdmans Publishing Co., 1963. Pp. xxxi+705.

Robertson, Archibald Thomas. *A Grammar of the Greek New Testament in the Light of Historical Research*. Nashville: Broadman Press, 1934. Pp. lxxxvi+1454.

_____. *Word Pictures in the New Testament*. 6 vols. Nashville: Broadman Press, 1930-33.

Smith, J.B. *Greek-English Concordance to the New Testament*. Scottdale, Pennsylvania: Herald Press, 1955. Pp. 430.

Vincent, Marvin R. *Word Studies in the New Testament*. 4 vols. Grand Rapids: Wm. B. Eerdmans Publishing Co., 1887.

Vine, W.E. *An Expository Dictionary of New Testament Words*. 4 vols. in 1. Old Tappan, New Jersey: Fleming H. Revell Co., 1940.

Wuest, Kenneth S. *Studies in the Vocabulary of the Greek New Testament*. Grand Rapids: Wm. B. Eerdmans Publishing Co., 1945. Pp. 149.

C. BOOKS AND COMMENTARIES

Barclay, William. *Flesh and Spirit*. Nashville: Abingdon Press, 1962. Pp. xiv+384.

_____. *The Promise of the Spirit*. London: The Epworth Press, 1960. Pp. 120.

Barndollar, W.W. *The Validity of Dispensationalism*. Des Plaines, Illinois: Regular Baptist Press, 1964. Pp. 70.

Barnes, Albert. *Barnes' Notes on the New Testament*. Grand Rapids: Kregel Publications, 1962. Pp. 1763.

Barnhouse, Donald Grey. *The Invisible War*. Grand Rapids: Zondervan Publishing House, 1965. Pp. 288.

Bonner, Gerald. *The Warfare of Christ*. London: The Faith Press, 1962. Pp. 122.

Bounds, Edward M. *Satan: His Personality and Overthrow*. Grand Rapids: Baker Book House, 1963. Pp. 157.

Bruce, F.F. *The Book of Acts*. Grand Rapids: Wm. B. Eerdmans Publishing Co., 1954. Pp. 555.

Bullinger, E. W. *The Two Natures in the Child of God*. London: Samuel Bagster & Sons, Ltd., 1970. Pp. 52.

Chafer, Lewis Sperry. *The Ephesian Letter*. New York: Loizeaux Brothers, Bible Truth Depot, 1944. Pp. 176.

_____. *Grace*. Grand Rapids: Zondervan Publishing House, 1922. Pp. xvi+373.

_____. *He That Is Spiritual*. Grand Rapids: Dunham Publishing Co., 1964. Pp. 192.

_____. *Satan*. Grand Rapids: Dunham Publishing Co., 1919. Pp. vii+180.

_____. *Systematic Theology*. 8 vols. Dallas: Dallas Seminary Press, 1948.

Culbertson, William. *God's Provision for Holy Living.* Chicago: Moody Press, 1957. Pp. 112.

Dunn, Jerry G. *God is for the Alcoholic.* Chicago: Moody Press, 1965. Pp. 205.

Edman, V. Raymond. *They Found the Secret.* Grand Rapids: Zondervan Publishing House, 1960. Pp. 159.

Gordan, S.D. *Quiet Talks About the Tempter.* New York: Fleming H. Revell Co., 1910. Pp. 249.

Gray, James M. *Satan and the Saint.* London and Edinburgh: Fleming H. Revell Co., 1909. Pp. 124.

Greenlee, J. Harold. *Introduction to New Testament Textual Criticism.* Grand Rapids: Wm. B. Eerdmans Publishing Co., 1964. Pp. 160.

Guthrie, Donald. *The Pauline Epistles.* London: The Tyndale Press, 1961. Pp. 319.

Haggai, John Edmund. *How to Win Over Worry.* Grand Rapids: Zondervan Books, 1959. Pp. 157.

Halverson, Richard C. *Christian Maturity.* Grand Rapids: Zondervan Publishing House, 1956. Pp. 137.

Harper, Michael. *Spiritual Warfare*. Plainfield, New Jersey: Logos International, 1970. Pp. 127.

Hogg, C.F., and W.E. Vine. *The Epistle to the Galatians*. Grand Rapids: Kregel Publications, 1921. Pp. viii+352.

Hunter, John E. *Living the Christ-Filled Life*. Zondervan Publishing House, 1969. Pp. 130.

Ironside, H. A. *Galatians*. New York: Loizeaux Brothers, Inc., 1941. Pp. 235.

Kent, Homer A., Jr. *The Pastoral Epistles*. Chicago: Moody Press, 1958. Pp. 320.

King, Guy H. *The Fellowship*. London and Edinburgh: Marshall, Morgan and Scott, Ltd., 1954. Pp. 127.

LaHaye, Timothy. *Spirit-Controlled Temperament*. Wheaton, Illinois: Tyndale House Publishers, 1966. Pp. 141.

Legters, Lil. *The Simplicity of the Spirit-Filled Life*. Philadelphia: Christian Life Literature Fund, 1930. Pp. 63.

Lightfoot, J.B. *The Epistle of St. Paul to the Galatians*. Grand Rapids: Zondervan Publishing House, 1957. Pp. xiv+384.

Macaulay, J. C. *Life in the Spirit*. Grand Rapids: Wm. B. Eerdmans Co., 1955. Pp. 112.

Mackintosh, C.H. *The Assembly of God*. Vol. III, *Miscellaneous Writings of C.H. Mackintosh*. Neptune, New Jersey: Loizeaux Brothers, 1898.

McClain, Alva J. *Law and Grace*. Chicago: Moody Press, 1954. Pp. 80.

McMillan, S.I. *None of These Diseases*. Westwood, New Jersey: Fleming H. Revell Co., 1963. Pp. 158.

Mead, Frank S. (ed.). *Encyclopedia of Religious Quotations*. London: Peter Davies, 1965. Pp. 534.

Narramore, Clyde M. *This Way to Happiness*. Grand Rapids: Zondervan Books, 1958. Pp. 176.

Nelson, Marion H. *Why Christians Crack Up*. Chicago: Moody Press, 1960. Pp. 125.

Pentecost, J. Dwight. *Your Adversary the Devil*. Grand Rapids: Zondervan Publishing House, 1969. Pp. 191.

Pickering, Ernest D. *Doctrine of the Holy Spirit*. Des Plaines, Illinois: Regular Baptist Press, 1971. Pp. 64.

Pink, Arthur W. *The Doctrine of Sanctification*. Swengel, Pennsylvania: Bible Truth Depot, 1955. Pp. 206.

Ridout, S. *The Person and Work of the Holy Spirit*. New York: Loizeaux Brothers, [n.d.]. Pp. 224.

Roush, H.L. *Henry and the Great Society*. Belpre, Ohio: By the author, 1969. Pp. 108.

Ryrie, Charles Caldwell. *Balancing the Christian Life*. Chicago: Moody Press, 1969. Pp. 191.

_____. *Dispensationalism Today*. Chicago: Moody Press, 1965. Pp. 221.

_____. *The Holy Spirit*. Chicago: Moody Press, 1965. Pp. 126.

_____. *The Place of Women in the Church*. New York: The Macmillan Co., 1958. Pp. xi+155.

Sanders, J. Oswald. *A Spiritual Clinic*. Chicago: Moody Press, 1958. Pp. 192.

Scofield, C.I. *The New Life in Christ Jesus*. Greenville, South Carolina: The Gospel Hour, Inc., 1915. Pp. 117.

_____. *Plain Papers on the Doctrine of The Holy Spirit.* Grand Rapids: Baker Book House, 1966. Pp. 80.

Simpson, A. B. *Wholly Sanctified.* Harrisburg, Pennsylvania: Christian Pub. Inc., 1925. Pp. 136.

Stam, Cornelius R. *True Spirituality.* Chicago, Illinois: Berean Bible Society, 1959. Pp. 209.

Stanford, Miles J. *Principles of Spiritual Growth.* Lincoln, Nebraska: Back to the Bible Broadcast, 1966. Pp. 104.

Stewart, James A. *Heaven's Throne Gift.* Philadelphia: Revival Literature, [n.d.]. Pp. xi+194.

Tasker, R.V.G. *The General Epistle of James.* Grand Rapids: Wm. B. Eerdmans Publishing Co., 1956. Pp. 144.

Tuggy, Joy Turner. *The Missionary Wife and Her Work.* Chicago: Moody Press, 1966. Pp. 191.

Unger, Merrill F. *The Baptizing Work of the Holy Spirit.* Findlay, Ohio: The Dunham Publishing Co., 1962. Pp. 147.

_____. *Biblical Demonology.* Wheaton, Illinois: VanKampen Press, Inc., 1952. Pp. 250.

Vincent, Marvin R. *The Epistles of Paul*. Grand Rapids: Wm. B. Eerdmans Publishing Co., 1946. Pp. xl+565.

Walvoord, John F. *The Holy Spirit*. Grand Rapids: Dunham Publishing Co., 1965. Pp. xx+288.

Westcott, Brooke Foss. *The Epistle to the Hebrews*. Grand Rapids: Wm. B. Eerdmans Publishing Co., 1970. Pp. lxxxiv+504.

Wright, Walter C. *Ephesians*. Chicago: Moody Press, 1954. Pp. 128.

Wuest, Kenneth. *Bypaths in the Greek New Testament*. Grand Rapids: Wm. B. Eerdmans Publishing Co., 1940. Pp. 124.

_____. *Ephesians and Colossians in the Greek New Testament*. Grand Rapids: Wm. B. Eerdmans Publishing Co., 1953. Pp. 254.

_____. *First Peter in the Greek New Testament*. Grand Rapids: Wm. B. Eerdmans Publishing Co., 1942. Pp. 135.

_____. *Galatians in the Greek New Testament*. Grand Rapids: Wm. B. Eerdmans Publishing Co., 1944. Pp. 192.

_____. *Golden Nuggets from the Greek New Testament*. Grand Rapids: Wm. B. Eerdmans Publishing Co., 1940. Pp. 122.

_____. *Great Truths to Live by from the Greek New Testament*. Grand Rapids: Wm. B. Eerdmans Publishing Co., 1952. Pp. 152.

_____. *Hebrews in the Greek New Testament*. Grand Rapids: Wm. B. Eerdmans Publishing Co., 1947. Pp. 271.

_____. *In These Last Days*. Grand Rapids: Wm. B. Eerdmans Publishing Co., 1954. Pp. 263.

_____. *The Pastoral Epistles in the Greek New Testament*. Grand Rapids: Wm. B. Eerdmans Publishing Co., 1952. Pp. 207.

_____. *Romans in the Greek New Testament*. Grand Rapids: Wm. B. Eerdmans Publishing Co., 1955. Pp. 300.

_____. *Treasures from the Greek New Testament for the English Reader*. Grand Rapids: Wm. B. Eerdmans Publishing Co., 1941. Pp. 131.

_____. *Untranslatable Riches from the Greek New Testament for the English Reader.* Grand Rapids: Wm. B. Eerdmans Publishing Co., 1942. Pp. 140.

White, Ernest. *The Way of Release.* Fort Washington, Pennsylvania: Christian Literature Crusade, 1947. Pp. viii+95.

D. PERIODICAL AND ENCYCLOPEDIA ARTICLES

Bellshaw, William G. "New Testament Doctrine of Satan," *Grace Journal*, IX (Fall 1968), pp. 24-39.

Elkland, O. "Formalism and Church Worship," *Moody Monthly*, LVII (November 1956), pp. 18-19, 89.

Lay, Berrne, Jr. "Upward!," *Reader's Digest*, March, 1958, pp. 223-24.

Toussaint, Stanley D. "The Spiritual Man," *Bibliotheca Sacra*, CXXV (April-June 1968), pp. 139-46.

Wuest, Kenneth S. "Victory Over Indwelling Sin in Romans Six," *Bibliotheca Sacra*, CXVI (January-March 1959), pp. 43-50.

Wilmington, H. L. "If I Were the Devil," *Baptist Bulletin* (December 1971), pp. 13-14.

E. UNPUBLISHED MATERIALS

Barrick, William Dennis. "In Eden, The Garden of God: A Study of Ezekiel 28:13." Unpublished Master of Divinity critical monograph, San Francisco Baptist Theological Seminary, 1971. Pp. iii+50.

Hodges, Zace C. "A Defense of the Majority-Text." Unpublished revised edition of a paper originally called "Introduction to the Textus Receptus," [n.d.]. Pp. 18. Mimeographed.

Sturz, Harry A. "The Use of the Byzantine Text-Type in New Testament Textual Criticism," [n.d.]. Pp. 288. Mimeographed.

About the Author

Warren Rushton has a degree in Mechanical Engineering. During his senior year at the Indiana Institute of Technology, he accepted Christ as his savior. He later graduated from Omaha Baptist Bible College, attended the Dallas Theological Seminary, and graduated with a Master of Divinity and a Master of Theology from the San Francisco Conservative Baptist Theology Seminary.

Loralea, his wife, is a nurse. They met in Bible college. They have been married for 54 years and have four children: Susan, Annmarie, Teresa, and Joshua. They also have nine grandchildren and two great-grandchildren.

Warren's ministry has been starting churches. While starting a church in Nebraska, he became State Chairman of the Nebraska Christian Home School Association. He published the *Home School Journal* and hosted Educational Insight, a radio program.

Warren still works as a mechanical engineer. He also teaches Bible classes and is a Bible Conference speaker.

CPSIA information can be obtained
at www.ICGtesting.com
Printed in the USA
FSHW011515081119
63802FS